ADAPTIVE INTELLIGENCE: EVOLUTIONARY COMPUTATION FOR NEXT-GEN AI

Saurabh Pahune

Mr. Kolluri Venkateswaranaidu

Dr. Sumeet Mathur

INDIA · SINGAPORE · MALAYSIA

ISBN 979-8-89699-191-5

PREFACE

The journey of writing this book, "Adaptive Intelligence: Evolutionary Computation for Next-Gen AI" originated from a genuine desire to understand how AI can go beyond conventional frameworks to tackle actual issues. As AI systems pervade almost every sector including clinical, transport, and social sectors it is important to know techniques that will enable these systems to learn, grow, and sustain themselves within the environments.

This book was born out of the authors' pool of experience gathered from professional practice over many years in various areas including data science, machine learning, and research. They compared that traditional AI techniques perform best in highly formalised circumstances, but the world's problems require self-evolving intelligent systems. In motivating the writing of this book, our intent went beyond simply cataloging these new research approaches and instead was to offer a reference work that both grounds these methodologies and shows how they can be applied.

This book caters for the researcher, student and professional who seeks to understand a blend of evolutionary computation and adaptive intelligence. That's why we've attempted to stay focused on key principles to provide readers with valuable information on how to properly work with these technologies.

This work is a comprehensive, or at least worthy, attempt to offer the basis for a reformist and elaborated, prospective enterprise. It looks at how intelligence has been defined and developed in the context of AI over time, assesses the relative merits of evolutionary computation compared with other approaches and examines issues of practical application from optimization to robotics. We try to explain the concepts in a simple manner but at the same time, exercise the readers' brain muscles when it comes to the possibilities of AI. The development of this book is a group effort, and we could not have accomplished it without the guidance of our families, teachers and the help of other people that we cooperated with. Through encouragement they supported us during numerous hours of research and writing.

Last but not least, we extend our gratitude to the reader who decided to follow us on this journey. It is our pleasure to encourage you not only to read this material but also to join the continuous development of the great area of adaptive intelligence.

DEDICATION

Mr. Himanshu Sinha

To my wife, children, and young learners who inspire and challenge me to contribute to the ever-evolving journey of learning and innovation.

Mr. Kolluri Venkateswaranaidu

This book is dedicated to all my family members, especially my parents who believed in me throughout my career. I would like to thank the researchers and scientists who inspired me for what I have become today

Dr. Sumeet Mathur

To my mother "Saroj", father "Roshan Prakash" my wife "Rashmi" and daughter "Rhythm", who never stopped believing in me

Acknowledgment

The creation of this book, "Adaptive Intelligence: Writing this paper titled "Evolutionary Computation for Next-Gen AI" has been quite an experience, and it has been my pleasure to write under the support of the following people and institutions.

Above all, we would like to thank our families for supporting us throughout the process of writing this book, for being there for our inspiration. To our spouses, parents, and children – Your support and faith in us during the time spent on researches and writings have been the bedrock of strength.

First of all we would like to express our deep appreciation to all mentors and educators who set fire to our desire in gaining knowledge and contributed to our further personal and career growth. They have provided us with great ideas and constant support throughout the understanding of the relations between artificial intelligence and evolutionary computation.

Gratitude to all the colleagues, partners, and the large scientific community as well. Communication of ideas, criticism as well as enthusiasm toward the development of AI and machine learning have been crucial in enhancing the content of this book. Particular recognition goes to those organizations and institutions that provide the access to the resources, data, and tools that were instrumental in this work.

We also thank the editorial and publishing teams for the excellent work in helping to turn our ideas into this finished product.

Organization, dedication, punctuality and attentiveness has been one of the best strengths we have seen.

Finally, we acknowledge you, the reader, for considering this work. We believe that this book enhances your knowledge of adaptive intelligence and evolutionary computation and motivates you to become part of this rapidly evolving area.

To all, who helped and encouraged us, we will always stay grateful. Thank you.

CONTENTS

Chapter 3: Theoretical Underpinnings | **106**

Chapter 4: Designing Evolutionary Computation Systems | **137**

CHAPTER 1

INTRODUCTION

1. Introduction

In the past ten years, AI and ML algorithms have been widely used in many different scientific fields, including engineering, physics, sociology, and biology. Indeed, cutting-edge methods have opened up exciting new possibilities in both academia and business. With its proven effectiveness in supervised and unsupervised machine learning tasks, the deep learning method family—which employs several kinds of ANN—has become the most consequential. With the proliferation of big, multi-domain datasets across many industries, researchers in the biomedical and healthcare sectors have taken a keen interest in using these methods for discovery science. In this case, practitioners may have access to thousands of possible predictors from which to build a model. Additionally, heuristics or rules-of-thumb for model training parameters might not be accessible when dealing with new challenges. This sort of less-or unrestricted learning environment is more typical in biological and biomedical science than in physical science or industrial applications, however it is not limited to these fields. When working with high-dimensional, heterogeneous biomedical data in a less-or unconstrained modelling context, three common problems often make it difficult to formulate optimised, effective AI/ML models.

The first thing that all the different kinds of AI and ML have in common is that practitioners need to use hyperparameters to optimise learning when they parameterise their designs. The outcomes and efficiency can be significantly impacted by these configuration parameters. Optimisation of learning hyperparameters and determination of when to terminate model training are two connected but distinct aspects of the problem. The current state of model training iterations is characterised by limited numbers of empirically chosen hyperparameters and frequent human tuning of these parameters. For example, in computational experiments, the majority of practitioners surveyed recently pursued 50 model fits or less. Manually searching for hyperparameters or using rules-of-thumb can be problematic when dealing with huge numbers or ranges of parameters because it affects reproducibility, produces suboptimal solutions, or becomes unworkable. Particularly infamous for their difficulty to "tune," or optimise, are deep learning models. Furthermore, due to the novelty of the problem, rules-of-thumb may not be applicable in discovery or early-stage science. There is mounting evidence that automated techniques of hyperparameter tuning outperform manual ones, and this has sparked a growing interest in creating such systems. In a perfect world, this kind of automated system would logically converge on an optimised solution by picking from a large pool of possible hyperparameter values.

2. Background and Motivation

One way to look about poverty is as a disease that needs a specific kind of medicine to be cured. People in poverty fight an uphill battle every day; poverty affects a sizable section of South Africa's population. Additionally, she stressed the significance of agricultural economic development, where various stakeholders may influence food security, rural development, and sustainable community building for the better. Specifically, for women and children living on farms, she emphasised that programs should work towards long-term improvements in their livelihoods. The North West Province (NWP) is home to a sizable farming population, yet many of these people, particularly the women who work the land, are unable to make ends meet. Since many women who work on farms do not have steady jobs, they are a drain on South Africa's coffers. These women also tend to have low levels of education.

Poverty in South Africa

Poverty is defined as "simply a state of being poor" in the Oxford Advanced Learner's Dictionary. People in poverty do not have access to resources that would help them overcome poverty, such as money, education, or social networks. Additionally, they do not earn enough money to pay for school, so they struggle to find work if they are illiterate or uneducated and cannot afford to send their children to school. There is a complicated web of relationships between poverty and chronic poverty in South Africa. One definition of chronic poverty, which is more common in rural regions, is the passing of poverty from one generation to another. South Africa's socioeconomic situation is impacted by this cycle of persistent poverty. Chapter Two presents a comprehensive analysis of South Africa's socioeconomic status, education and skills, unemployment, the NWP situation, and poverty management.

Income-generating projects (IGPs) and the link to motivation of participants

In order to improve the general well-being of low-income communities, sustainable projects are required. Despite efforts to reduce poverty through income generating projects (IGPs), many of these initiatives have failed or are not sustainable because of a lack of buy-in from relevant stakeholders. Nobody knows why there's no dedication. More study into IGP involvement, especially among women, is something that Madiand Mokgotho have called for.

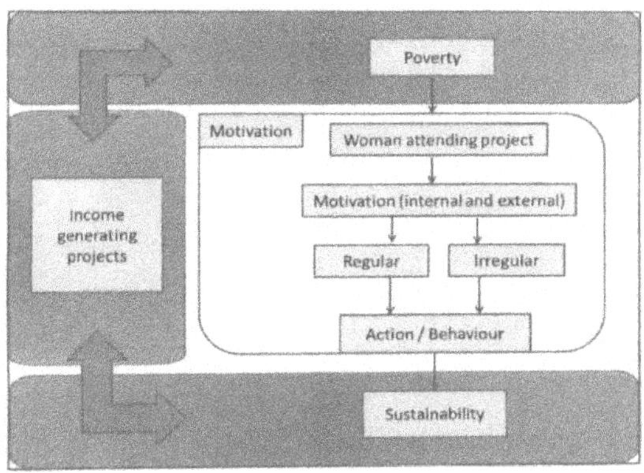

Source:- (Nasir et al., 2024)

characterise an individual's motivation as the strong impulse to respond to a demand or stimuli. The recognition of a need gives rise to tension, and the subsequent desire to alleviate this tension motivates the individual to do some sort of action. Therefore, the purpose of this research is to examine how women act in relation to their reasons for taking part in an IGP.

2.1. Evolution of Intelligence in AI

From its humble beginnings as a science-fictional idea to a game-changing engine propelling technical progress across industries, artificial intelligence (AI) has gone a long way. Science has advanced at a dizzying rate, and the quest to create AI that can mirror human intelligence has been an unrelenting priority. Coming full circle, this article will trace the fascinating history of AI, from its infancy to its present-day status as a revolutionary force in our contemporary society.

- **The Origins of Artificial Intelligence**

  Artificial intelligence (AI) has its origins in the groundbreaking 1950s work of visionaries like Alan Turing and John McCarthy. In order to determine whether a machine can mimic human behaviour, Turing devised the now-famous "Turing Test" and popularised the idea of machine intelligence. The Dartmouth Conference, which McCarthy spearheaded, is widely regarded as the academic institution that first introduced artificial intelligence (AI). This was the first step in the field of artificial intelligence, with early initiatives concentrating on learning, reasoning, and problem-solving.

- **Early Milestones in AI Development**

  During the 1950s and 1960s, researchers in artificial intelligence made significant strides. By creating the Logic Theorist, the first AI program to be able to prove mathematical theorems, Allen Newell and Herbert A. Simon demonstrated the promise of artificial intelligence. Additionally, machine learning and pattern recognition were made possible by Frank Rosenblatt's

1958 presentation of the notion of neural networks. In the decades that followed, AI made strides with the help of expert systems, which drew on the expertise of subject matter specialists to resolve difficult problems. New developments in robotics and natural language processing have significantly broadened the application of AI. Problems with technology and the notorious "AI winter" of the 1970s and 1980s, when interest and investment in artificial intelligence plummeted owing to unrealistic expectations, slowed development.

- **The Rise of Machine Learning and Big Data**

Thanks to improvements in machine learning algorithms and an abundance of data, artificial intelligence had a renaissance in the 1990s. Artificial intelligence systems were able to learn from past mistakes and gradually become better thanks to machine learning methods like supervised and unsupervised learning. The exponential growth of data and the proliferation of online resources have enabled groundbreaking developments in areas such as computer vision, natural language processing, and speech recognition by providing opportunities to train artificial intelligence models on massive datasets.

- **The Deep Learning Revolution**

Revolutionary advances in deep learning techniques, particularly CNNs and RNNs, sparked a new era in artificial intelligence. Using deep learning models, we were able to see incredible results in areas such as picture identification, language translation, and even defeating human chess and Go champions. The training and deployment of deep learning models were expedited by the availability of powerful computer resources, together with breakthroughs in parallel processing and hardware.

- **The Current State and Future Prospects**

These days, artificial intelligence (AI) is everywhere, impacting many parts of our daily life. A wide range of applications are being revolutionised by AI, including recommendation systems, driverless vehicles, virtual assistants, and healthcare diagnostics.

Areas including explainable AI, quantum computing, and reinforcement learning are anticipated to benefit from future AI developments. Integral to the development of AI in the years to come will be ethical concerns, such as measures to reduce bias and protect personal information.

2.2. Historical Context of Evolutionary Computation

Python is a highly popular programming language among developers due to its versatility and user-friendliness. Advanced algorithms and solutions can be more easily developed with the help of the supplied frameworks and tools. Python is particularly well-suited to evolutionary computation.

To solve challenging optimisation problems, evolutionary computation uses natural selection and genetics. Evolutionary computing includes genetic algorithms. With Python's extensive ecosystem of modules and tools, developers may easily implement these algorithms to find the best solutions for various challenges. This post will teach you the basics of evolution and genetic algorithms and show you how to use Python to apply them.

Understanding Evolution

To make sense of genetic algorithms in Python, one must have a firm grasp of evolutionary theory. Over time, organisms undergo a process known as evolution, which shapes them and allows them to adapt to their surroundings. It relies on a number of processes, including variation, natural selection, and reproduction. As time passes, a species will inevitably become better as a result of the increasing chances of beneficial individuals surviving and passing their genes on. This is a fundamental premise of evolution.

Genetic Algorithms: The Building Blocks

Biological evolution is the driving force behind genetic algorithms (GAs), an evolutionary application in computer science. They use genetic operators including mutation, selection, and crossover, as well as a population of possible solutions, to enhance the answers iteratively.

- **Population Initialization** – Building a gene pool is the initial stage of any genetic algorithm. Each individual represents a possible solution to the present problem.

- **Fitness Evaluation** – The fitness function is a measure of how well an individual solves problems. The solution's quality is graded according to specific criteria.

- **Selection** – In a move reminiscent of natural selection, the process gives an advantage to those who have higher fitness ratings. Selection procedures commonly used in tournaments and roulette wheels.

- **Crossover** – Genetic material from two selected individuals is mixed during the crossover process in order to create a new generation. This procedure facilitates both the exploration and utilisation of the solution space.

- **Mutation** – Mutation allows new possibilities to arise in a population by randomly altering an individual's genetic code. It discourages extinction-level convergence and promotes variety maintenance.

- **Termination Criteria** – Upon hitting a certain threshold, such as a predetermined number of iterations or a satisfactory outcome, the algorithm will exit.

Implementing Genetic Algorithms in Python

Python offers a wide variety of frameworks and tools that simplify the process of building genetic algorithms. A few popular libraries include PyEvolve, DEAP, and PyGAD. Take a look at the DEAP library implementation as an example.

- **Installing DEAP** – Get the DEAP library installed first by utilising your preferred package manager or pip.

- **Defining the Issue** – Use a genetic algorithm to zero in on the problem that needs fixing. Exact details regarding the goal function and any limitations are required.

- **Creating the Individual** – Detail the way in which a data structure (such a string or a list) stands in for a specific answer.

- **Implementing the Operators** – To find out how fit someone is, you need to define the evaluation function. Put the selection, crossover, and mutation operators into action with the help of the DEAP tools.

- **Configuring the Algorithm** – Pick the population size, number of generations, variation and selection operators, and so on.

- **Running the Algorithm** – Begin by populating the population with initial values. Then, iteratively apply selection, crossover, and mutation. Finally, end the algorithm based on the termination criteria.

- **Analysing the Results** – Look at what the algorithm came up with, put the best ones in order, and then figure out what they mean in relation to the problem.

<u>Enhancing Genetic Algorithms in Python</u>

An approach to betterment is known as "niching." Nicholing promotes diversity in a population by maintaining many subpopulations. Therefore, the algorithm can avoid converging to local optima too fast while exploring the solution space. Using niching strategies such as fitness sharing or crowding can make things more engaging and boost the chances of obtaining many good solutions.

By implementing adaptive parameter control, genetic algorithms can be further enhanced. Factors like population size, mutation rate, and crossover rate are typically employed as inputs. Adaptive parameter control, however, makes real-time adjustments to these parameters while the algorithm runs. This modification might be based on the characteristics of the population or the evolution of the algorithm. The algorithm can optimise its settings for better performance using approaches like GAAP and SAGA, which stand for Self-Adaptive Genetic Algorithms.

By implementing adaptive parameter control, genetic algorithms can be further enhanced. Factors like population size, mutation rate, and crossover rate are typically employed as inputs. Adaptive parameter control, however, makes real-time adjustments to these parameters while the algorithm runs. This modification might be based on the characteristics of the population or the evolution of the algorithm. The algorithm can optimise its settings for better performance using approaches like GAAP and SAGA, which stand for Self-Adaptive Genetic Algorithms.

Genetic algorithms are able to resolve difficult optimisation problems by employing robust methodologies. Python is an excellent platform for genetic algorithm implementation due to its user-friendly syntax and rich library ecosystem. Several problems can be efficiently addressed by developers by applying the principles of evolution and genetic operators.

The essay delves into the basics of evolution and genetic algorithms, showing how to use the DEAP module in Python to apply them. Insights like this will allow computer scientists to apply genetic algorithms to real-world problems and evolutionary algorithms to solve problems in different areas. The app's compatibility with genetic algorithms paves the way for boundless creative problem-solving opportunities.

2.3. The Need for Adaptive Intelligence

Some people don't understand how presidents can be so completely ineffective and yet manage to be re-elected or very nearly do so. Do you share my perplexion at the behaviour of voters who profess to have excellent hearing and vision but cast ballots for candidates who have already been demonstrated to be ineffective?

Tragically, those who back utter flops aren't limited to naive voters. A lot of people in the US and elsewhere are doing the same thing, but they're focussing on students who fared poorly on standardised exams instead of potential presidents.

When have standardised exams been ineffective? In any case, it's the same as having ears and eyes that work together. Worldwide, intelligence quotients increased by 30 points in the twentieth century, a phenomenon known as the Flynn effect. Just what did 30 IQ points buy the world? No, I don't mean the capacity to change with the circumstances, or adaptable intelligence. There will soon be no turning back the clock on global warming. A number of countries' leaders—including those in the US, Canada, Australia, and Russia—are likely to have average intelligence but are causing significant harm to the environment. Nearly seven million individuals are losing their lives every year due to air pollution. Liberal governments swept the globe after WWII, but now we're witnessing an upsurge of tyrants and would-be dictators who are gaining power through legitimate elections rather than coups. Forty percent or more of America's waterways are too dirty for fishing. Annually, 36,000 Americans lose their lives and 100,000 are wounded due to gun violence. A lot of them are little kids. (Contrast this with the 249 firearm-related deaths in Canada in 2018.) Just what are American students learning in the classroom? With an increase in IQ of 30 points, what exactly did the nation gain? Even though the US is fighting an authoritarian trend in leadership, IQs are still on the rise.

Regardless of how helpful it may be in predicting culturally valued outcomes like GPA, on-time graduation, college acceptance, job placement, and performance, among others, as citizens of the United States or any other nation or the world, we must all consider the possibility that what we have termed "general intelligence" is not a silver bullet, or even a partially useful solution, for our society's problems. On the contrary, it has diverted our attention to irrelevant abilities at an inappropriate moment. Anyone can claim, "we've been had," but in that case, they're claiming it all on their own.

Articles and publications like the now-infamous The Bell Curve cite correlational evidence that makes IQ tests sound like good indicators of future achievement in many fields. There ought to be some predictive value to them, I suppose, but it's overstated. It is possible to achieve this distortion in four different methods.

The first issue is that correlations are usually adjusted for "restriction of range," which makes it seem like the findings are valid for the "full" population instead than one with a limited set of skills. Naturally, the complete population is and ought to be a mystery. Is it inclusive of cultures that place a higher importance on soft skills than on IQ? Does it encompass everyone whose adaptive needs are primarily related to subsistence hunting and gathering, political acquiescence (like the present administration in the United States), or religious obedience?

Because of this, every single successful person in the workforce and every single successful college student was a man. A logical conclusion was drawn from this: they were "men's jobs." No woman could accomplish them. A opportunity was obviously never offered to the women. A lot of people did not have a fair shot at success, including Blacks, Chinese, Jews, and those with disabilities. Finally, the results of the correlational research would confirm what everyone already knew: that members of the disrespected groups had a lower rate of success. Is it reasonable to hold the "success" of students at New York City's Stuyvesant High, which has very high test scores, up to that of kids at Wadleigh Secondary School for the Visual & Performing Arts, a school that has very low test scores? Are their chances of success equal?

In conclusion, we have created a system of psychometric self-fulfilling prophecies that enables the privileged to justify their privilege in their own minds. At the same time, a large portion of the globe is descending into chaos. Instead than wasting time and energy on general intelligence problems that don't matter, we should put our attention on adaptive intelligence that can solve real-world challenges (Schrader, 2020).

3. Evolutionary Computation vs. Traditional AI Techniques

What is evolutionary computation?

A subfield of AI, evolutionary computation finds extensive application in continuous optimisation and other difficult optimisation issues.

When dealing with issues with more variables than classical algorithms can manage, evolutionary computation techniques are employed. For the aim of tackling such complicated problems, these computer models make use of evolutionary algorithms, which basically employ evolutionary processes. They base their models on evolutionary principles such as natural selection, which involves passing on characteristics from the most successful models to subsequent generations, and inheritance from successful models of earlier generations.

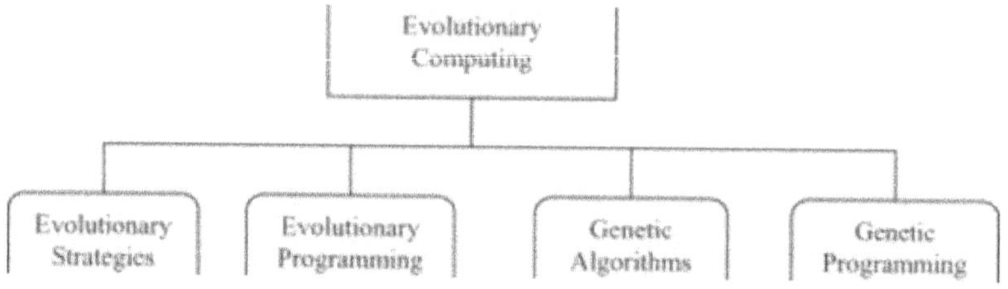

Sources : (Llanes et al., 2016)

Why do we use evolutionary computation?

Evolutionary algorithms see heavy application in the field of computer science due to their remarkable capacity to generate highly optimised solutions for various challenges. For certain data formats and families of problems, there are even variations that are developed and utilised exclusively.

Evolutionary biologists also make use of this subfield of AI when investigating overarching patterns in evolutionary processes.

What are the types of evolutionary algorithms?

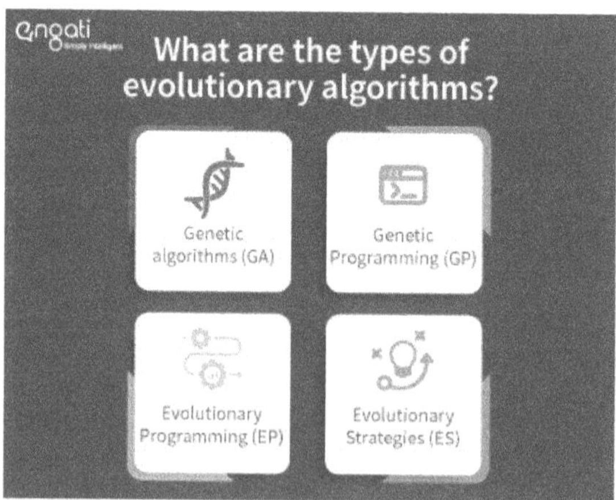

Sources: (SrmiSTAdmiNrmp, 2024)

There are various types of evolutionary algorithms. Here are the most significant ones:

1. **Genetic algorithms (GA)**

   Among evolutionary algorithms, genetic algorithms are by far the most used. Problems are solved as strings of numbers by them. Binary strings predominate, although the best ones often reveal something regarding the issue at hand.

   Operators such as mutation and recombination are employed by these algorithms. On occasion, they'll use both operators simultaneously.

   Genetic algorithms can help choose the best set of parameters from which to construct a prediction model. Deciding which variables to include is essentially an optimisation and combinatory problem.

   One great thing about genetic algorithms is that they can build upon previous successes to find the optimal solution. Over time, it enhances the selecting process.

   The basic premise of genetic algorithms is to iteratively combine different solutions in order to extract the best genes or variables. In the end, it aids in developing more suitable persons.

   Parameter hyper-tuning, function maximum/minimum determination, and neural network architectural search (Neuroevolution) are other applications of genetic algorithms. Use it for feature selection as well.

   Genetic algorithms (GA) work by iteratively combining the best solutions after generating a small number of random solutions representing various variables. Choosing the best responses in a generation (selection), creating two new individuals (cross-over) from the genes of the solutions (mutation), and randomly tweaking an individual's genes (cross-over) are the three primary stages of a genetic algorithm.

2. Genetic Programming (GP)

Software programs are the solutions to these problems. Their ability to resolve computational problems is what determines the fitness of these computer programs.

An automated programming technique that promotes the creation of computer programs that solve or nearly solve issues is known as Genetic Programming (GP). Basically, it's a way to "breed" programs by making incremental improvements to a randomly generated collection of code.

Stochastic program change and selection according to some established quality criteria allow for improvements. Basically, genetic programming systems allow programs to grow in order to solve machine learning and automatic programming difficulties that have been previously stated.

Hill climbing is a typical term for genetic programming's underlying heuristic search technique. Finding the best program, or even a good one, from the space of all programs is what it entails.

3. Evolutionary Programming (EP)

Genetic programming is a good analogy here. Evolutionary programming, on the other hand, allows numerical parameters to change over time while optimising systems with fixed structures.

In 1960, Lawrence J. Fogel began experimenting with this evolutionary algorithm paradigm in an effort to develop AI through the use of simulated evolution as a learning process. Predictor machines with finite states were developed by him. As it stands, there is no set structure or representation for evolutionary programming; rather, it is a broad computational dialect. Evolutionary programming and evolutionary methods are starting to blend into one another.

Mutation is the primary operator in evolutionary programming. Instead of considering all population members to be of the same species, evolutionary programmers classify them according to a specific species. Each parent produces a new generation using a survivor selection process that consists of ($\mu + \mu$).

4. **Evolutionary Strategies (ES)**

Utilising self-adaptive mutation rates is a common tactic in evolutionary methods. They represent solutions using vectors of real values.

The principles of evolution provide the basis of evolutionary strategies, which are optimisation methods. Mutation and selection are their primary search operators, and they employ natural representations that rely on the problem. A generation is an iteration of the loop that applies the operators. The iterative process keeps on until some end condition is satisfied. In contrast to evolutionary strategies, which operate at the behavioural level, most evolutionary algorithms operate at the genetic level.

An individual's genes are not linked to their physical expression because it is coded directly.

By taking this route, we may establish a robust causation, whereby a little shift in the coding results in a little shift in the individual and vice versa.

3.1. Comparative Analysis of Evolutionary Algorithms and Classical AI Methods

Nowadays, there is a significant growth in the complexity of practical applications. Complex and difficult-to-solve problems plague several fields, including robotics, data mining, bioinformatics, decision-making, operation research, and many more. Evolutionary computations is a hypothesis that attempts to solve such complicated problems by drawing on ideas from Darwinian natural evolution. The term "Evolutionary Algorithms" (EAs) describes a class of algorithms used in evolutionary computing. To find answers to difficult, real-world problems, EA use simulated evolution. When heuristic methods are impractical or produce subpar outcomes, evolutionary processes are the way to go. EA is attracting a lot of attention, especially because of its practical problem-solving applications. In the last 20 years, evolutionary algorithms have grown in popularity as a technique for optimisation, searching, and solving difficult issues. The idea of gradual change over time, as proposed by Darwin in his theory of evolution, is a major influence. The underlying ideas are as follows: there is a population or populations of persons vying for a finite supply of resources. The population is constantly evolving, and it will always be exploring the universe of potential shapes (the fitness landscape) to find the most adapted individuals.

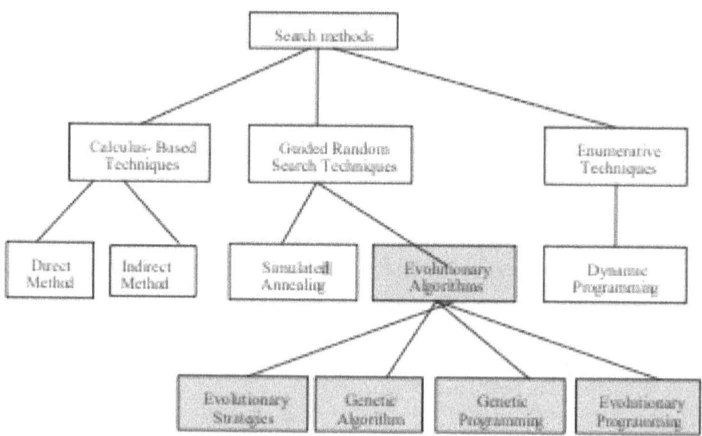

Sources : (Silaich & Gupta, 2023)

Evolutionary algorithm

The evolutionary algorithm (EA) is a type of broad stochastic search method that falls under the umbrella of evolutionary computation. Figure 1 displays EA's position in various search algorithms. Based on the idea of population optimisation, it is a metaheuristic optimisation algorithm. In order to do partial searches, metaheuristics are higher-level procedures that seek out, generate, or choose heuristics or lower-level procedures. It works for a wide range of optimisation problems when there isn't enough data or processing power to solve them properly. It offers a satisfactory answer in those cases.

The processes of natural selection, mutation, recombination, and reproduction serve as models for EAs. In order to maximise the quality function, a set of potential solutions that are members of the function domain are generated at random. A quality function, here represented as an abstract fitness function, is then applied to the problem area. We can select the most promising individuals for the following generation by utilising the fitness function. The best approach would be to use mutation and/or recombination to achieve this goal. To symbolise recombination, the binary operator is used. It generates a new collection of candidates (the children) by applying this operator to an existing set of candidates (the parents). Another possibility is that a single offspring is born when a mutation occurs in just one parent.

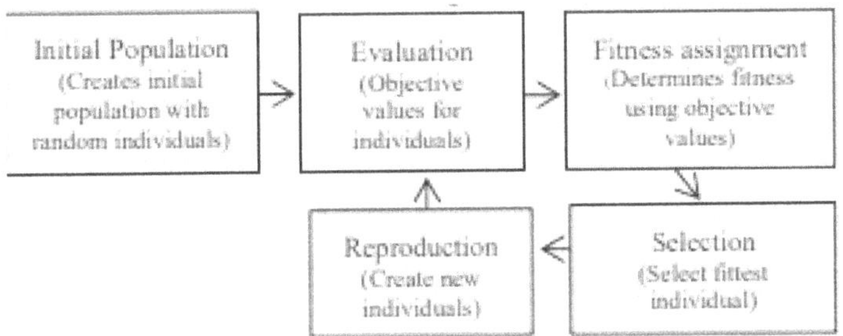

Source: - (Moretti et al., 2024)

<u>**Steps involved in solving the problem with EA**</u>

- **Step 1:** The first stage is to identify the problem space and the space for fixing it. What we call it is representation. This is the environment where change occurs. One reason for representation is to help connect the dots between the actual world and the EA environment. The phenotypes are the things that make up the potential solutions in the original issue space. Genotypes are the matching encodings of the people within EA.

- **Step 2:** It entails figuring out assessment Activity (Fitness Assessment). The selection process is based on this function, and it allows for improvements.

- **Step3:** Once the population's representation is defined, a solution may be found. A multi-step genotyping process creates the evolutionary unit.The number of individuals in a given representation is called its population.

- **Step 4:** Parental selection determines the individuals' quality. This ensures that the following generation is headed by responsible adults. An organism changes in order to produce new generations if it is chosen to be a parent.

- **Step 5**: To make new operators out of existing ones, variation operators are used. Recombination and mutation are the two main operators for variation. Represents mutation, the unary operator. When administered to a single genotype, it produces offspring with that genotype. A binary operator, on the other hand, is recombination. During recombination, the genetic material from two or more parents is mixed to create a new genotype or genotypes in the progeny.

- **Step 6:** Individuals are differentiated according to their quality through the process of survival selection. The process of choosing a parent is very similar to this. However, this occurs at various points throughout evolution. This process is carried out solely in cases where certain parents produce offspring.

- **Step 7**: A initial population is created using individuals that are generated at random. Forming an initial population typically involves using specific heuristics with greater fitness. Assuming the problem is aware of the optimal fitness level, the process can be terminated upon attaining this level. However, due to its stochastic nature, EA cannot ensure the achievement of an ideal solution.

<u>**Types of EAS**</u>

Among the many subfields that make up evolutionary algorithms are genetic algorithms, evolutionary strategies, genetic programming, and evolutionary programming. The underlying premise of all EAs is the simulation of individual evolution through mutation, selection, and reproduction. However, its implementation and problem-specific application are key differentiators.

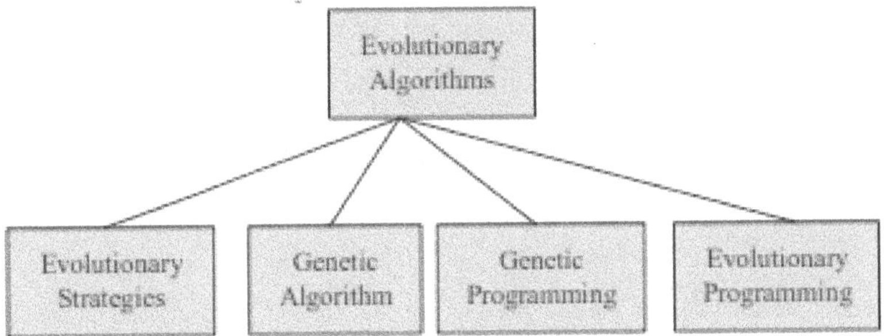

Source: - (Vikhar, 2024)

- **Genetic algorithm (GA):**

  GA has grown popular as a kind of EA because it provides the most accurate representation of the bio-inspired evolution process. Machine learning, pattern identification, and optimisation problems frequently make use of it. Its primary applications are adaptive system design and adaptive search, and it was initially suggested in 1970 by Holland and his student.In order to solve preexisting crimes, GA employs recombination and mutation operators. The end product is a numerical bit-string that displays the genes.

- **Genetic programming**

  In 1992, Koza created it. Unlike GA, which uses universal binary coding to describe qualities, genetic programming uses sets of instructions or programs as attributes. Solutions are thus constructed by GP in the manner of computer programs. Using a fitness function, one can determine if a system is capable of solving a computational issue. Thanks to genetic programming's tree-based encoding, it's useful in many domains, including arithmetic, mathematical functions, boolean operations (such AND, OR, and NOT), recursive functions, and more.

- **Evolution strategy**

  In 1973, Rechenberg initially suggested the evolution technique as a way to optimise complex, multimodal, non-differentiable functions. By eliminating unnecessary code, it solves the real expression of an attribute. So, the evolution technique employs self-adaptive mutation rates and represents solutions as real-valued vectors. Routing and networking, biochemistry, optics, and engineering design are a few well-known areas where evolution tactics are used.

- **Evolutionary programming**

  For the purpose of developing AI, Fogel initially proposed the idea of EP in 1966. The way it operates is quite similar to how Evolutionary Strategies operate. It is not limited in how data types and properties can be used, unlike ES. Although EP's program structure is static, the numerical parameters are free to change. Evolutionary programming has useful applications in forecasting, generalisation, games, and automatic control, among others.

Advantages of Evolution ARY Algorithm

EAs have been widely used in many complex problem-solving applications, due to its many advantages over classical search and optimization techniques.

- As it is inspired by natural evolution, it is conceptually simple and flexible.

- It utilizes prior information. It is obvious that the method that considers prior information about problem will outperform a method using less information and it will also restrict the search space.

- Some numeric techniques available are only applicable for applications having continuous values or other having constrained sets. But EA is representation independent.

- Evolution is a parallel process. Each evaluation in performs parallel operations and only operations

- performed during selection process requires some serial processing.

Extensions to EAS

Local search heuristics are those that take a person's characteristics into account. A memetic algorithm (MA) combines elements of both EA and local search. Individuals in nature attempt to adapt to their environments by changing their traits after birth. The term for this kind of change is plasticity. Anyone can acquire such flexibility in EA, and the means by which individuals are chosen for adoption are completely at random. You can change the relative importance of the local search and EA methods at random. This allows the EA to be extended to MA, which will execute the local search heuristic's good multi-start search.

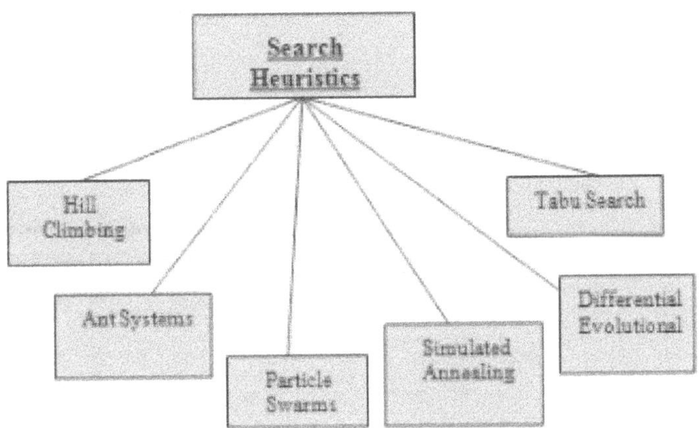

Source: - (Vikhar, 2024)

3.2. Strengths and Weaknesses of Evolutionary Computation

Evolutionary Computation (EC) is a class of optimization algorithms inspired by the principles of natural selection and genetics. Here's a breakdown of its strengths and weaknesses:

1. **Strengths:**

   - **Global Optimization:** EC algorithms are good at searching large and complex solution spaces, which makes them suitable for global optimization problems where traditional methods may get stuck in local optima.

- **Adaptability:** These algorithms can be adapted to a wide range of problems without requiring significant changes to the underlying method. They can handle non-differentiable, noisy, and multi-modal functions.

- **Exploration of Large Search Spaces:** EC performs well when the search space is vast and unknown, as it explores multiple regions simultaneously due to its population-based nature.

- **Parallelism:** Since the algorithms evaluate many individuals in a population at once, EC is naturally suited for parallel and distributed computing environments, which can significantly reduce computation time.

2. **Weaknesses:**

- **Computationally Expensive:** EC methods often require a large number of function evaluations, especially when working with large populations or complex problems, which can make them slow to converge.

- **Premature Convergence:** Although EC generally explores diverse solutions, there is still a risk of premature convergence to local optima, especially if the algorithm's diversity mechanisms aren't robust enough.

- **Problem-Specific Tuning:** EC algorithms often require careful tuning of parameters (e.g., mutation rates, population size, selection mechanisms) for optimal performance, and finding the right configuration can be challenging.

- **Lack of Guarantees:** Evolutionary algorithms do not guarantee finding the global optimum, particularly within a fixed number of generations. There's always a trade-off between exploration and exploitation.

4. Overview of Adaptive Intelligence

On a personal and institutional level, modern businesses face enormous challenges. Recruiting new team members, creating training to improve skills, accommodating some employees' "requirements" for remote work, and implementing programs to engage and retain employees all contribute to a healthy and productive organisation. A rapidly emerging component of building and maintaining an agile organisation system is ubiquitous learning, which entails cultivating both individual and collective knowledge. The ability to quickly adjust to new situations is a fundamental competency that leaders should cultivate through effective learning and the development of flexible, scenario-based knowledge. Numerous internal and external pressures are exerted on businesses. Change that is both revolutionary and long-lasting must be able to adapt, according to the research. Problems and even danger can arise in any organisation when factors like employee turnover, falling sales, and inefficient marketing all play a role. The capacity to develop and foster flexible and adaptive abilities, as well as a clear mission and vision from leadership, are essential for the long-term success of any endeavour. Adaptability, according to an essay by McKinsey & Co. published in August 2021, is the key to success in the face of hardship. Consistent with this idea, adaptability hinges on "memory"—that is, a thorough understanding of the past is essential for guiding the present and future in scenario analysis, transformation planning, and the development of measurable strategies for success.

Organisational Sustainability On both the individual and ecological levels, adaptability is paramount. Having the flexibility to adjust to different work settings is a great source of motivation and concentration. As an example, it's not hard to find evidence that companies can be successful in non-domestic locations. Uniqlo in the US, Starbucks in China, Fiat in South America, and Caterpillar in India. On the flip side, environmental control has far-reaching, beneficial consequences for a company's long-term viability. Many companies in the modern athletic consumer goods industry have shifted their focus from workout apparel to related but distinct categories, such as golf and tennis, by rebranding themselves with new items. An incredibly successful example of this is

Under Armour. Additionally, companies with the ability to discover or build new settings have a better chance of sustaining and growing in new markets with innovative products and services. The recent decision by the Amazon "juggernaut" to sell its own line of products under its own brand name (Blink) is one such example.

Additionally, we undergo selections of new markets to pursue in our pursuit of revenue growth. As an example, our company's present product offerings do not allow us to serve customers in Europe. Are there any ways we may improve the design and functionality to meet the demands of consumers in Spain and Germany? Workplace communities, their maintenance, and the promotion of change can all benefit greatly from the use of technology. Work teams can become more productive, effective, and agile with the help of enhanced back-office solutions, regardless of whether the organisation decides to introduce more IT or adopts new methods to IT administration. Achieving desirable results for a company relies heavily on the smart use and implementation of these so-called systems. Actually, IQ, emotional intelligence, and social psychology all come together to form adaptive intelligence. appeal to the concept of "social circuitry" as a way to encourage behavioural modification. Within the domain of intelligence development, there is a nascent phase characterised by the adoption of new strategies, methods of interacting with others, and boundaries. People seek to leaders who are "socially smarter" who can effectively adjust to new situations and pressures to boost their own and their teams' performance.

Communication abilities are another commonly held belief about what a leader must have. The three Ps of look, listen, and learn are at the heart of a new strategy. If you want the best possible results, following the correct sequence of these steps is essential. Together, AI and the adage "seeking to understand before you are understood" make a strong case. Leadership, in particular, is responsible to the organisation in this regard, "The leader is endowed to protect and nurture those who seemingly are in distress - educate, train and empower," writes Fioravante (2021). The key is for leaders to see what their team members are capable of and invest the time and energy needed to develop it.

4.1. Definition and Scope of Adaptive Intelligence

What we call "Adaptive Intelligence" in the context of artificial systems is their ability to take in data from their surroundings, process it, and then change its behaviour accordingly. With adaptive intelligence, systems may learn and adapt from their experiences and the world around them, rather than operating according to static algorithms or pre-defined rules.

Definition:

Adaptive Intelligence can be defined as: The ability of a system to dynamically adjust its decision-making process or behavior in response to varying external stimuli or environments, often without explicit human intervention. These systems are capable of learning and self-optimization, making them more resilient and flexible than static systems.

Scope:

The scope of adaptive intelligence encompasses a wide range of applications and methodologies, covering various aspects of learning, evolution, and adaptation within AI systems. It includes the following key elements:

1. **Autonomous Learning:** Adaptive systems are designed to learn from data, experiences, and their interactions with the environment. This learning process can be supervised, unsupervised, or reinforcement-based, depending on the nature of the problem.

2. **Self-Optimization:** These systems are capable of optimizing their performance by adjusting their parameters or strategies in real-time. Self-optimization is particularly valuable in dynamic environments where conditions and objectives may shift unpredictably.

3. **Flexibility and Resilience:** Adaptive intelligence provides systems with the flexibility to handle uncertainty and change. This resilience allows them to continue functioning effectively even when faced with unforeseen challenges, such as disruptions in the environment or changes in objectives.

4. **Evolutionary Processes:** Many adaptive systems incorporate evolutionary principles, such as genetic algorithms or evolutionary strategies, which allow them to evolve solutions over time. These systems can generate novel behaviors or strategies that were not explicitly programmed, mimicking the process of natural selection.

5. **Human-Environment Interaction:** Adaptive intelligence often extends beyond the digital realm, playing a role in human-computer interaction (HCI), robotics, and autonomous systems. These systems can adapt to human behavior, preferences, and feedback, leading to more personalized and effective interactions.

In summary, adaptive intelligence represents a shift towards more dynamic, evolving AI systems that can handle complexity and uncertainty with greater autonomy. It emphasizes learning, adaptation, and optimization in diverse environments, making it a key concept in the development of next-generation AI solutions.

4.2. Key Characteristics of Adaptive Systems

Good, straightforward stories are loved by humans. From Steve Jobs to Superman, we adore heroes. Hero of the future. This man, you know, who's so good at making the perfect call at the perfect moment. The hero who rescues everyone. Hope is essential for everyone. That being said, we are all ardent believers in this guy's existence.

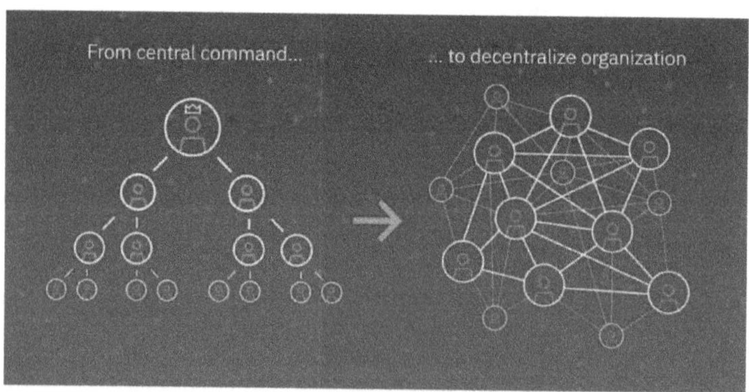

Source: - (Søreide, 2024)

Good, simple narratives are cherished by people. We love heroes, whether they are Steve Jobs or Superman. A future hero. This individual, you know, has an uncanny knack for predicting when to make the right decision. All are saved by the hero. Every person needs hope. Having said that, we are all firm believers in the presence of this man.

The idea for the Cynefin framework was proposed by Dave Snowden. The tool is helpful in determining the nature of the problem. Chaos, disorder, complexity, and obviousness are the five states it suggests. Looking around, you'll see that a lot of things are complicated. So is the economy. Everyone knows that healthcare is complicated. In addition to the economy, schools, safety nets, etc. Everything under the sun.

For many of us, COVID has brought complexity into sharp focus. Would we betray our economy if we kept people at home? Should we open the floodgates and slaughter hundreds—if not millions—of people? What can we do to put a stopped to it? Continued thereafter. This is a dead end for us. No definitive solutions have bcen provided. Why? For the simple reason that it is an adaptive system of great complexity. An evil dilemma. No matter how much we wish there were, the answers are elusive.

What are some of the key characteristics of a complex adaptive system?

Things don't follow a straight path. There are numerous different pieces that work together. You can do that on your own. There isn't a governing body. A change in one condition of one of these components can cause a domino effect to occur in other parts, with results that aren't always predictable. Mutual reliance. Consequently, the system state is dynamic and unpredictable. Its condition will never recur, unless by chance, as Snowden says. So, it follows that using historical data to construct models is useless.

It is also futile to try to analyse a complicated system. You can't change the system by taking a reductionist approach and dismantling it. According to Russel Ackoff, the progenitor of systems thinking, a complex system is not just the sum of its parts' attributes. None of its constituents possess the qualities that manifest in it. Take the human body as an example of a complicated adaptive system. The city's traffic infrastructure is very flexible and intricate.

The only way to deal with a complex system is to interact with it.

Do some testing, take some measurements, study the results, then do it all over again. We are completely unable to foretell its future condition. All we can do is attempt to sway it. But it won't be able to plan its future form. Most emergent processes are hard to predict.

What does it say about experts?

"Experts are experts of the past," is a common saying among Jack Ma, the Chinese billionaire, entrepreneur, and man who was unable to secure even a basic position at KFC. Experts have a firm grasp of the components. What about their effects on the environment and the network, though?

The Chinese entrepreneur and millionaire Jack Ma often says, "Experts are experts of the past," in reference to his many failures to get even the most entry-level job at KFC. Experts have a firm grasp of the components. What about their effects on the environment and the network, though?

With COVID, we hear from experts every day who make claims that are later revealed to be incorrect. Many false beliefs about who we are are constructed by our ego. Our educational institutions have conditioned us to know what to say and how to answer correctly. We all pretend all the time, even when we really don't know. Complications test the mettle of any professional.

And what about the leader?

Most intriguing is the tendency of a complex system that is disorderly to seek order. In a beehive, no one is in command. Nonetheless, a hierarchy forms. The bees are not hardwired to seek out any one kind of bloom. What we term it is autopoiesis. Stigmergy is a distributed coordinating mechanism that the system employs in its pursuit of homeostasis, an evolutionary condition that maximises efficiency.

Consider for a moment a world in which humans have complete command over the actions of every single bee in a beehive.

Do you think that we could make the system more efficient at producing honey?

Probably you're thinking, "not a chance," just like I am. But we act as though we can perfect complicated systems. We act as if certain leaders have the requisite knowledge of a complicated system to find a solution. No matter how complicated the problem is, whatever "solve" means.

The Lean Startup methodology, created by Eric Ries, is something that Dave Snowden is fond of pursuing. It argues there is no scientific proof and labels it as a belief. When Snowden asked Ries about failing enterprises, Ries had to know. With a "no, why?" came the response. Why? Because Snowden did it when working at IBM, and they discovered that unsuccessful businesses were mimicking the strategies of successful ones. Depressing.

No leader resists any complex system, as the COVID 19 has been demonstrating.

Everything is gone. Plus, their failure rate increases in direct proportion to their linear thinking. Simplicity is not a friend to complexity.

An antiquated hierarchical method is inadequate for managing the increasingly efficient information society brought forth by networkization. Gone is the myth of the leader. To discover levers that cause systems to evolve, only teams can hope. The term "holistic expert" does not apply to any one person. Even tomorrow can't be taught from the past (Mignon, 2020).

We humans are hardwired to make judgements as a group. The leader passed away in 2020, thus now is the time for political systems and business management to embrace complexity and collective intelligence. He was afflicted with COVID. In the words of Moises Naim, "Power, as we knew it is over" (The End of Power).

4.3. Examples of Adaptive Intelligence in Practice

Adaptive Intelligence (AI) has been on our minds for some time. To review, artificial intelligence is the process of sharing data in real-time in order to obtain authoritative knowledge that is suited to the situation and helps businesses maximise value.

Customer insights (CI) clients are telling us in more and more advisory, workshops, enquiries, and FLB sessions that building adaptive intelligence capabilities would help them handle a plethora of other challenges as well. For example:

- A systematic data innovation approach encourages knowledge sharing throughout the organization, reduces data acquisition redundancies, and brings energy and creativity to the CI practice.

- A good handle on data origin kickstarts your marketing organization's big data process by providing a well-audited foundation to build upon.

- Better data governance and data controls improve your privacy and security practices by ensuring cross-functional adoption of the same set of standards and processes.

- Better data structure puts more data in the hands of analysts and decision-makers, in the moment and within the systems of need (eg, campaign management tools, content management systems, customer service portals, and more).

- More data interoperability enables channel-agnostic customer recognition, and the ability to ingest novel forms of data — like preference, wearables data, and many more — that can vastly improve your ability to deliver great customer experiences.

- A solid data product management team can really elevate the visibility and value of customer insights by turning CI from a cost center into a revenue-generating organization.

That is to say, leaders in consumer insights may future-proof their CI organisation by setting in motion the processes to become adaptively intelligent.

Check out a sample assessment down below; we just released a tool to help you gauge your AI preparedness. To help you get from where you are now to where you want to be, it evaluates seven different types of competence and gives you advice on what to do next. Share the test with as many people as possible, and use the results to inform your strategy for achieving adaptive intelligence. And don't hesitate to set up an inquiry to go over the findings—I always recommend it!

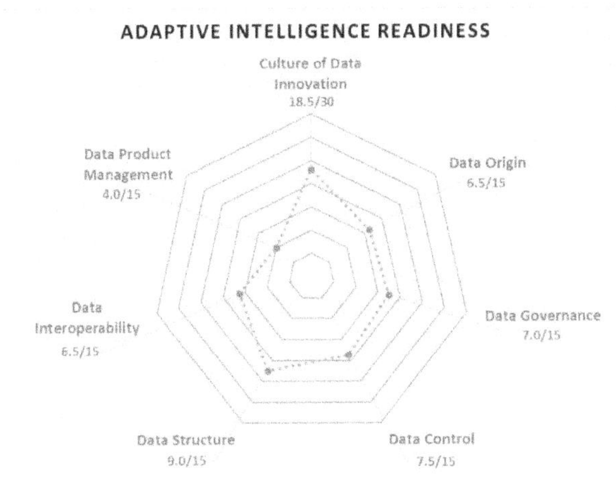

Source: - (Matchaya et al., 2024)

5. *Relevance of Evolutionary Computation in Modern AI*

Evolutionary computation (EC) plays a significant role in modern AI, contributing to various aspects of machine learning, optimization, and problem-solving. Its relevance continues to grow as AI faces increasingly complex challenges. Here's an overview of how evolutionary computation is influencing modern AI:

1. Optimization

- **Hyperparameter Tuning:** Machine learning models' hyperparameters are optimised with the use of evolutionary algorithms (EAs). Optimal configurations can be more efficiently explored by EAs than by conventional grid or random search methods in complex, high-dimensional search spaces.

- **Neural Architecture Search (NAS):** Automatic neural network creation is a complex and time-consuming process; EAs play a crucial role in this process by optimising the depth, structure, and connectivity of neural networks.

2. **Evolutionary Algorithms for Reinforcement Learning (RL)**

- **Genetic Algorithms (GAs) in RL:** Evolutionary strategies like GAs are used in RL to optimize policy and value functions. Evolutionary methods can sometimes be more efficient than gradient-based methods, especially in non-differentiable environments.

- **Neuroevolution:** This is a technique where neural networks are evolved using EAs. It's particularly useful in scenarios where traditional training methods, like backpropagation, struggle, such as in sparse reward environments.

3. **Handling Complex Problem Spaces**

- **Optimization Problems:** EAs excel at solving complex, multimodal optimization problems where traditional methods struggle due to local minima. Modern AI applications in fields like robotics, logistics, and finance benefit from these robust optimization techniques.

- **Robustness and Flexibility:** Evolutionary computation can handle a wide variety of constraints and objectives, making it useful in real-world scenarios with uncertain, dynamic environments. For instance, evolutionary robotics uses EAs to evolve control strategies for robots in unpredictable environments.

4. **Interpretable AI**

- **Symbolic Regression and Genetic Programming:** EAs are used in symbolic regression to find interpretable models or equations that describe data. This contrasts with deep learning models, which are often seen as black boxes. Genetic programming, an EC technique, helps generate human-readable models that are easier to interpret.

- **Fuzzy Logic Systems:** Evolutionary algorithms optimize fuzzy logic systems, which can provide interpretable decision-making models.

5. Evolution-Inspired Deep Learning Techniques

- **Neural Network Regularization:** Evolutionary algorithms inspire regularization techniques in deep learning, such as dropout and mutation-based approaches that introduce variation and prevent overfitting.

- **Training Ensembles:** Evolutionary algorithms are also used to train ensembles of models, selecting and evolving diverse models that together improve performance over a single model.

6. Bio-Inspired AI

- **Swarm Intelligence and Multi-Agent Systems:** Techniques like Particle Swarm Optimization (PSO) and Ant Colony Optimization (ACO), derived from biological evolution, contribute to AI for tasks such as distributed problem-solving and multi-agent coordination in dynamic environments.

- **Co-Evolution:** Co-evolutionary algorithms, where multiple species evolve simultaneously and influence each other's fitness, are applied in game AI, adversarial networks, and scenarios requiring competitive and cooperative strategies.

7. Sustainability and Scalability

- **Efficient Resource Usage:** EC techniques are often computationally less demanding than deep learning methods, especially when dealing with small datasets or resource-constrained environments. This makes them a sustainable choice for certain AI applications, particularly when resources like computational power are limited.

- **Scalable Solutions:** Evolutionary algorithms are highly parallelizable, making them scalable across distributed computing platforms, cloud environments, and even specialized hardware like GPUs and TPUs.

8. **Automated AI Development**

- **AutoML:** EC is used in automated machine learning (AutoML) pipelines to evolve and optimize machine learning models with minimal human intervention. This allows for quicker deployment of AI solutions tailored to specific tasks.

- **Creative AI:** Evolutionary algorithms contribute to creative AI applications such as generating art, music, and designs. The exploration and exploitation balance in EC is particularly suited for these tasks, where novelty and diversity are desired outcomes.

Evolutionary computation remains highly relevant in modern AI due to its ability to tackle complex optimization problems, enhance reinforcement learning, contribute to interpretable AI, and provide scalable, bio-inspired solutions. As AI continues to evolve, the role of evolutionary computation is likely to expand, particularly in areas that require flexibility, robustness, and creativity.

5.1. Current Trends in AI and Evolutionary Computation

Artificial Intelligence (AI) and Evolutionary Computation are evolving rapidly, fueled by advances in machine learning, computing power, and theoretical innovations. Here's an overview of the current trends in both fields:

1. **Neuroevolution and Evolutionary Reinforcement Learning (ERL)**

   Neuroevolution refers to the use of evolutionary algorithms to optimize neural network architectures, hyperparameters, or weights. With the rise of deep learning, neuroevolution has gained attention as an alternative to gradient-based methods.

Evolutionary Reinforcement Learning (ERL) combines evolutionary algorithms with reinforcement learning. In ERL, evolutionary algorithms optimize policies or hyperparameters, while reinforcement learning refines them. This hybrid approach is becoming popular for solving complex control tasks, such as robotic manipulation.

2. Automated Machine Learning (AutoML) and Evolutionary Search

Feature selection, algorithm selection, and hyperparameter optimisation are all steps in the process of generating machine learning models that AutoML tries to automate.

Evolutionary computation techniques, such as Genetic Algorithms (GA) and Particle Swarm Optimization (PSO), are increasingly used for searching large, complex model spaces, enabling AutoML systems to generate high-performing models without manual intervention.

3. Generative AI and Evolutionary Creativity

The rise of Generative AI (e.g., GPT-4, DALL-E) has sparked interest in using evolutionary algorithms for creative tasks, such as generating art, music, or text.

Evolutionary algorithms can be used to evolve creative outputs by iterating over generations of potential solutions, scoring them based on their novelty or aesthetic appeal. This combination is leading to innovations in creative AI applications.

4. Multi-Objective Optimization

Multi-objective evolutionary algorithms (MOEAs) are being widely adopted to solve problems involving trade-offs between competing objectives. These algorithms are finding applications in areas like energy optimization, finance, and logistics.

Emerging approaches are focusing on improving the scalability and efficiency of MOEAs, enabling them to tackle higher-dimensional and more complex problems.

5. Co-Evolution and Open-Ended Evolution

Co-evolutionary algorithms involve multiple populations evolving together, with their fitness functions dependent on each other's performance. This is useful for applications like game AI, where agents evolve strategies against each other.

Open-ended evolution explores the continuous generation of novel and complex behaviors without a predefined goal, inspired by biological evolution. This approach is applied in areas like autonomous robotics and generative design.

6. AI for Evolutionary Computation

Machine learning techniques are being integrated with traditional evolutionary algorithms to improve their performance. For example, deep learning models can be used to guide the search process in evolutionary algorithms, or to predict the fitness of potential solutions, thereby reducing the computational cost.

Similarly, AI methods are being used to analyze the behavior of evolutionary systems, helping to identify patterns, predict outcomes, and improve optimization processes.

7. Quantum Evolutionary Algorithms

Researchers are investigating quantum iterations of evolutionary algorithms as quantum computing advances. It is believed that some groups of problems, like optimisation and cryptography, could be solved substantially more quickly by these Quantum Evolutionary Algorithms (QEA) than by standard evolutionary algorithms.

These trends reflect the growing synergy between AI and evolutionary computation, where each field enhances the capabilities of the other. The future of this intersection promises more sophisticated, autonomous, and adaptable systems across a wide range of applications.

5.2. The Role of Evolutionary Algorithms in Addressing Modern Challenges

A family of optimisation methods known as evolutionary algorithms (EAs) draws inspiration from natural selection, mutation, and crossover, among other evolutionary ideas. These algorithms have become popular because they can tackle complicated, multidimensional problems that are hard to solve with more conventional approaches. EAs play a crucial role in addressing several modern challenges across various fields, including industry, healthcare, environmental management, and artificial intelligence. Here's a detailed look at their role in tackling these challenges:

- **Optimization in Complex Systems**

  o **Industry and Engineering:** Many industries face optimization problems where the solution space is vast and traditional methods are inefficient. EAs are particularly useful in complex engineering design, scheduling, and logistics. For example, in manufacturing, evolutionary algorithms help optimize production processes by finding the best configuration of machines, minimizing waste, and maximizing throughput. In transportation, EAs assist in optimizing routes and schedules to reduce fuel consumption and emissions.

  o **Finance:** In financial modeling and trading, evolutionary algorithms can optimize portfolios by selecting the best combination of assets under various constraints. They are also used in algorithmic trading to evolve trading strategies that can adapt to market conditions over time.

- **Healthcare and Biomedical Applications**

  o **Drug Discovery and Development:** The process of discovering new drugs involves searching through a massive space of possible chemical compounds. EAs help in optimizing this search by simulating the evolutionary process, selecting promising compounds for further study.

These algorithms can also optimize the combination of drugs in multi-drug therapies, such as those used in cancer treatment.

- **Medical Diagnosis:** Evolutionary algorithms are used to develop models that can accurately diagnose diseases by analyzing complex medical data. For example, they can optimize neural networks used in medical image analysis to improve the detection of conditions like cancer, heart disease, or neurological disorders.

- **Sustainability and Environmental Management**

  - **Renewable Energy Optimization:** EAs play a vital role in optimizing the design and operation of renewable energy systems, such as wind and solar farms. They help in finding the best configuration of turbines, panels, and energy storage systems to maximize efficiency and minimize costs. Additionally, evolutionary algorithms can optimize the scheduling of energy distribution in smart grids to balance supply and demand in real-time.

  - **Environmental Monitoring and Management:** In environmental management, EAs are used to optimize models for monitoring pollution, managing natural resources, and designing sustainable agricultural systems. For example, they can help optimize irrigation schedules to conserve water while maximizing crop yields.

- **Artificial Intelligence and Machine Learning**

  - **Neural Network Optimization:** Evolutionary algorithms are increasingly being used in machine learning, particularly in optimizing the architectures of neural networks. This approach, known as neuroevolution, allows for the automatic design of network structures that can outperform those designed manually. Neuroevolution is especially valuable in situations where the optimal network architecture is not known in advance, such as in reinforcement learning and game AI.

- o **Robotics:** In robotics, evolutionary algorithms are used to optimize robot behaviors and control strategies. By simulating evolutionary processes, these algorithms can generate efficient movement patterns and decision-making strategies for robots operating in complex environments, such as autonomous vehicles or robotic surgery.

- **Tackling Global Challenges**

  - o **Climate Change Mitigation:** Addressing climate change involves solving complex problems like reducing carbon emissions, optimizing renewable energy systems, and managing environmental resources. Evolutionary algorithms assist in these efforts by optimizing strategies for carbon capture, energy efficiency, and sustainable land use.

  - o **Disaster Management:** EAs help in developing optimal strategies for disaster response and recovery. They are used to simulate and optimize evacuation plans, resource allocation, and rebuilding efforts in the aftermath of natural disasters such as hurricanes, earthquakes, and wildfires.

- **Security and Cybersecurity**

  - o **Threat Detection:** Evolutionary algorithms are used in cybersecurity to detect anomalies and potential threats in network traffic. They help optimize intrusion detection systems by evolving detection rules that can adapt to new types of attacks.

  - o **Cryptography:** In cryptography, EAs assist in optimizing encryption algorithms and breaking cryptographic codes by searching through large spaces of possible keys or configurations.

6. Chapter Summary

This chapter delves into the intersection of evolutionary computation and adaptive intelligence within the broader context of artificial intelligence (AI). It begins by introducing the core concepts, providing readers with an understanding of the motivation behind the integration of evolutionary techniques in AI systems.

Background and Motivation: The chapter highlights the evolution of intelligence in AI, tracing its development from traditional methods to more sophisticated adaptive approaches. It discusses the historical context of evolutionary computation, a field inspired by biological evolution, which has emerged as a crucial tool for developing intelligent systems. The section emphasizes the need for adaptive intelligence in AI, where systems must be able to learn, adapt, and evolve in response to dynamic environments.

Evolutionary Computation vs. Traditional AI Techniques: This section provides a comparative analysis between evolutionary algorithms (EAs) and classical AI methods. The advantages and limitations of evolutionary computation are explored, showcasing how it differs from traditional AI techniques in areas like flexibility, adaptability, and problem-solving efficiency. The strengths of EAs, such as their ability to explore large solution spaces, are weighed against their weaknesses, such as computational cost and convergence speed.

Overview of Adaptive Intelligence: Here, the concept of adaptive intelligence is defined, outlining its scope within the AI landscape. Key characteristics of adaptive systems, such as learning from experience, self-organization, and resilience to changing conditions, are explained. The section also includes examples of adaptive intelligence in practice, illustrating how evolutionary computation is applied in real-world scenarios to solve complex problems that require adaptability and flexibility.

Relevance of Evolutionary Computation in Modern AI: The final section discusses the relevance of evolutionary computation in the current AI landscape. It examines modern trends in AI, such as the rise of deep learning and reinforcement learning, and how evolutionary algorithms complement these approaches. The role of EAs in addressing contemporary challenges in AI, including optimization, robustness, and innovation, is highlighted, showcasing their continued importance in advancing the field.

Overall, this chapter establishes a foundation for understanding the synergy between evolutionary computation and adaptive intelligence, emphasizing their importance in creating resilient, adaptive AI systems capable of tackling complex, real-world problems.

Part 1: (Very Short Questions)

1. What is the significance of the evolution of intelligence in AI?

2. How did evolutionary computation emerge in a historical context?

3. Why is adaptive intelligence needed in modern AI systems?

4. How do evolutionary algorithms compare to traditional AI techniques?

5. What are the strengths and weaknesses of evolutionary computation?

6. How is adaptive intelligence defined, and what is its scope?

7. What are the key characteristics of adaptive systems in AI?

8. Can you provide examples of adaptive intelligence in real-world applications?

9. What are the current trends in AI-related to evolutionary computation?

10. How do evolutionary algorithms help address modern AI challenges?

Part 2: (Short Questions)

1. What is the significance of adaptive intelligence in the evolution of AI?

2. How does evolutionary computation compare to traditional AI techniques?

3. What are the key characteristics that define adaptive intelligence systems?

4. How are evolutionary algorithms used to solve modern AI challenges?

5. What are the strengths and weaknesses of evolutionary computation in contrast to classical AI methods?

Part 3: (Long Questions)

1. How has the evolution of intelligence in artificial intelligence (AI) systems paralleled the historical development of evolutionary computation, and why has there been a growing need for adaptive intelligence in contemporary AI applications?

2. In what ways do evolutionary algorithms differ from traditional AI techniques, and what are the comparative advantages and disadvantages of evolutionary computation when applied to complex problem-solving scenarios?

3. What is adaptive intelligence, and what are the key characteristics that distinguish adaptive systems from other forms of artificial intelligence? How can adaptive intelligence be applied effectively in real-world scenarios?

4. What role does evolutionary computation play in addressing modern AI challenges, and how do recent trends in AI research and development shape the relevance of evolutionary algorithms in today's technological landscape?

5. Given the strengths and weaknesses of evolutionary computation, in what areas of modern AI do evolutionary algorithms hold the most promise, and where might they face limitations in scaling or performance compared to other AI techniques?

Part 4: (MCQs)

1. Which of the following best describes the evolution of intelligence in AI?

   a. The gradual development of AI systems that can adapt to their environment

b. A fixed set of rules programmed into an AI

c. The elimination of human involvement in decision-making

d. The use of deep learning algorithms only

2. What is the primary focus of evolutionary computation in the historical context?

   a. Replicating human reasoning

   b. Solving optimization problems using techniques inspired by natural evolution

   c. Developing rule-based expert systems

   d. Enhancing traditional machine learning algorithms with more data

3. Why is adaptive intelligence important in AI?

   a. It allows systems to learn and adjust to changing environments

   b. It replaces human intelligence completely

   c. It focuses on static, non-changing tasks

   d. It is used to train supervised models

4. Which of the following is a strength of evolutionary computation compared to traditional AI techniques?

   a. Better handling of highly structured data

   b. Ability to search large and complex solution spaces

   c. Faster training times

   d. Simplicity in implementation

5. Which of these is NOT a characteristic of adaptive intelligence?

   a. Learning from experience

   b. Flexibility to changing environments

   c. Fixed behavior based on programmed rules

   d. Capability to improve over time

6. Which of the following is an example of adaptive intelligence in practice?

    a. A chess-playing algorithm using predefined moves

    b. A spam filter that updates its criteria based on user feedback

    c. A sorting algorithm working with static data

    d. A calculator performing arithmetic functions

7. What is one of the weaknesses of evolutionary computation when compared to traditional AI techniques?

    a. Difficulty in handling dynamic environments

    b. Inefficiency with large, complex datasets

    c. Tendency to get stuck in local optima

    d. Inability to process structured data

8. Which of the following best represents the role of evolutionary algorithms in addressing modern AI challenges?

    a. Providing efficient solutions to NP-hard problems

    b. Replacing neural networks entirely

    c. Serving as a direct alternative to reinforcement learning

    d. Optimizing hyperparameters in machine learning models

9. What is a key distinction between evolutionary computation and traditional AI techniques?

    a. Evolutionary algorithms use pre-programmed knowledge

    b. Traditional AI techniques rely on rule-based systems, while evolutionary algorithms mimic natural selection

    c. Evolutionary algorithms are faster to train than traditional AI models

    d. Traditional AI is focused on optimization problems

10. Which of the following current trends highlights the relevance of evolutionary computation in modern AI?

    a. Increased use of rule-based expert systems

    b. Growth in solving complex optimization and machine learning problems

    c. Reducing the need for data pre-processing

    d. Decline in research on evolutionary algorithms

Answer

1	2	3	4	5	6	7	8	9	10
a	b	a	b	c	b	c	d	b	b

CHAPTER 2

FOUNDATIONS OF EVOLUTIONARY COMPUTATION

7. Introduction

Figure 1 depicts the main features of an evolutionary algorithm. The term "fitness criterion" refers to the method of evaluating a set of potential answers to an issue. These solutions are like parents to their children. These progenies are produced by means of mutations, recombination, or other random processes on the parents. The solutions compete for survival and the chance to become parents to the next generation by scoring the offspring. With the exception of artificial life research that aim to discover emergent qualities of simulations and a few extended varieties of evolutionary computing, such particle swarm and ant colony approaches, this core protocol or variants of it appear in almost all evolutionary algorithms. Many fields, including health, bioinformatics, military planning, scheduling, and forecasting, have found success with this basic evolutionary method in the last 20 years, with varied expansions. Worldwide, the field of evolutionary computing is likely to see the publication of over 3,000 publications per year.

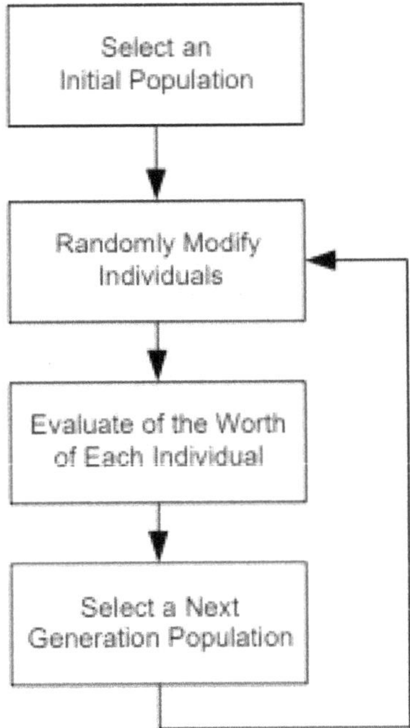

Source: - (Fogel, 2010)

Over the past 55 years, evolutionary computation has come a long way. Some of the first ancestors of those people can be traced back twenty years earlier. As an example, Cannon1 pointed out in 1932 that evolution was essentially a learning process, drawing direct parallels to how people learn. The "obvious connection between [machine learning] and evolution" is another point made by Turing2. Computer simulations of evolution were already a popular concept by the mid-1950s. A robot learning to navigate an arena was the subject of one of the earliest theoretical studies on simulated evolution. Machines that can think, including those that can play chess, could be designed using mutation and natural selection, according to Friedman3,4.Campbell5,6,7 also put forth the idea in the late 1950s and 1960s that learning and evolution are closely related.

Tragically, the evolutionary computation community is mostly unaware of these historical contributions and perhaps most other early contributions as well. This ignorance stems from a lack of thoroughness and reflects the field's relative youth in comparison to, example, chemistry, physics, or mathematics. There were a lot of novel attempts at evolutionary computing in the early days of computers. We currently possess the computational capacity to delve deeper into these ground-breaking concepts. The goal of this review paper is to perhaps inspire such initiatives. Though they may not receive the same level of attention in popular literature as, say, trade magazines, this study aims to shed light on less well-known historical contributions to artificial life, genetic system modelling, evolving programs, and developing hardware. It goes on to say, based on what we know now, what the future holds for evolutionary algorithms. Space constraints prevent us from providing adequate coverage to all pioneering and underappreciated endeavours. Fogel19 addresses these points for interested readers.

8. *Historical Development*

The rise of Europe as a global economic powerhouse with relatively high living standards was not an accident. Because of its cultural and geographical characteristics, this area has historically been favoured by global development events. Ideas, philosophy, and organisation were brought to southern Europe by the Greeks. Democracy was advocated by Greek philosophers. The Romans elevated the idea of empire to unprecedented heights. During their dominion of much of Europe and North Africa from 150 BCE to 475 CE, the Romans unified many ideologies. A standardised network was brought to Europe by the Roman Empire. The Romans built a network of highways, bridges, aqueducts, and ports that allowed them to reach every corner of their vast empire. They were able to control an empire. By capitalising on the strongest points of whatever area they ruled over, they allowed the most talented craftspeople to concentrate on their strengths. The result was the emergence of a market economy and product specialisation. Making one's own food was a thing of the past. In the market, they might sell their wares and buy goods from other people, the quality of which would exceed what they could create at home. Due to local resources or specialised skills, regions that specialised in certain items could convey those goods to markets far away. Between southern Europe and North Africa, the Roman Empire stretched.

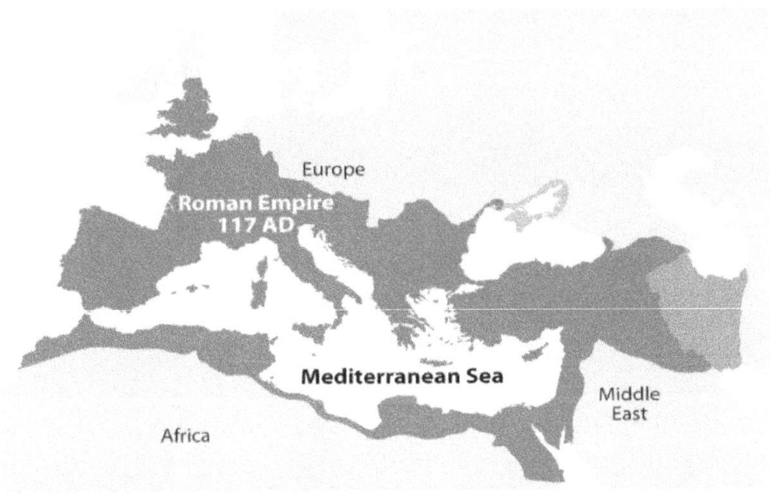

Source: - (Royal Berglee, 2016)

It is a common misconception that the Vikings from Scandinavia (Norway, Sweden, and Denmark; 900-1200 CE) were a gang of renegade raiders who looted and pillaged northern Europe. They may have been fierce fighters on the battlefield, but behind the scenes they were adept artisans, farmers, and dealers. They established trade channels all over the northern hemisphere. The Vikings made advantage of Europe's waterways for transportation, drawing on their extensive maritime knowledge and expertise. From Russia to Iceland and possibly North America, they were the first to build the northern world. In what is now Canada, Greenland, and Iceland, they established colonies. The adaptability and seafaring prowess of their longships were well-known. All the way to Constantinople at Constantinople, the Vikings advanced deep into Europe. The Byzantine Empire reportedly used Vikings from Scandinavia as mercenaries.

Colonialism

A new age of thought, innovation, and development did not begin in Europe until the Dark Ages came to an end. Changes throughout

Europe and the globe were sparked by the Renaissance in the late fifteenth century. Columbus sailed the three ships across the Atlantic Ocean in 1492, finally touching down on American shores. The period of European colonialism, which began with this event and only faded after WWII, began with this event. The European nations that still have colonies or protectorates bear the scars of colonialism. Governments' efforts to regulate commerce and encourage the rapid accumulation of riches through the extraction of precious metals from their colonies were key components of the mercantilist economic theory that provided the impetus for colonialism.

The Agrarian Revolution

A lot of innovations in agriculture that affected food production in Europe happened after the Renaissance. New technology substantially improved agricultural output, which had previously relied on labour-intensive and rudimentary methods. The introduction of new technologies such as ploughs, seeders, and harvesting tools prompted changes in land ownership and reform policies. These developments paved the way for the growth of port cities, which in turn facilitated the development of urban markets for agricultural excesses. The potato, brought back from the colonies by colonial ships, changed the face of crop production forever. The agricultural revolution describes the dramatic changes that occurred during this time in terms of farming technology. Industrial innovations like the steam tractor and steel implements, which were ushered in by the agrarian revolution, greatly enhanced agricultural output on a global scale.

The Industrial Revolution

Being an island nation, Great Britain was able to dominate the oceans by building the greatest navy in the world. They colonised a vast area that included what is now Australia and what is now Canada. An industrial era that altered human product production began in the late 1700s in northern England, when the Industrial Revolution was launched. Smelting iron, using steam engines to generate electricity, switching to coal as an energy source, and the idea of mass production all altered the production process.

Source: - (Royal Berglee, 2016)

The invention of the steam engine made it possible to generate power on the go. One early form of hydropower was the use of waterwheels driven by swiftly moving rivers or streams. The mobile engines of industry were propelled full speed forward by coal as fuel and steam as power. Woven fabric was created from raw materials like wool and cotton using power looms. Anywhere at any time, a power loom driven by a steam engine could do its weaving. Industrialisation, facilitated by abundant and inexpensive raw resources and labour, bestowed immense riches on the countries and individuals at the head of the industrial revolution.

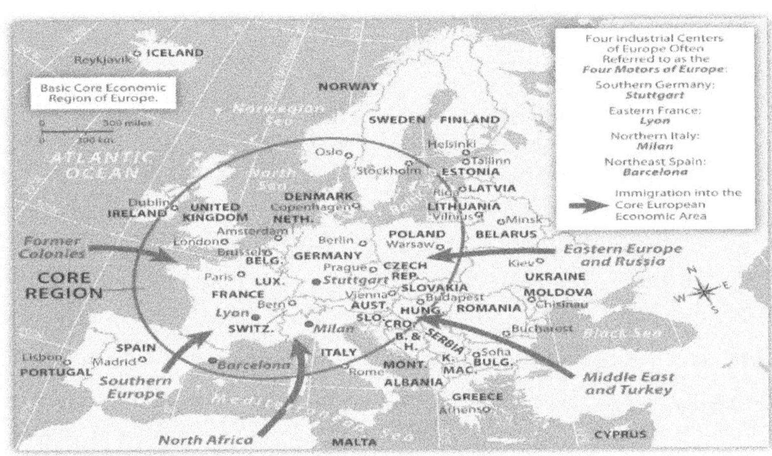

Source: - (Royal Berglee, 2016)

Industrial port cities were the primary sites of urbanisation in Europe. Raw materials might be imported by ships, manufactured by factories, and then exported by ships. These events gave rise to what is now known as the central business district (CBD). Everyone had to congregate in one area for business purposes because walking was the primary means of transportation. Factories and port facilities have to be adjacent to banks, retail shops, food markets, and residential units. Europe is home to some of the world's most densely populated urban areas, which sprang out of the continent's rapid industrialisation.

The capital of many European nations is smaller than the main metropolis, which is more than twice as big. Cities that are twice as large as their second city and serve as outstanding examples of national pride and history are considered primate cities. The capital of a nation is not necessarily the same as the primate city, despite the common misconception to the contrary. New York metropolis, for instance, is the most important metropolis in the United States, even if Washington, DC, is the capitol. Primate cities are representations of a nation's character and history, and they also serve as symbols of that country's persona. Even though they are frequent, not every country has a primate city. Industrialisation fuelled the rise of primate cities like London, Rome, and Paris, which now serve as financial and commercial hubs. Primate cities are generally situated on or near large rivers or serve as ports.

8.1. Early Algorithms and Concepts

Ideas in Algorithms John A. Musser Osman, BrianMay 16, 2003 With the help of graduate research assistants Brian Osman, Michael LaSpina, and Mayuresh Kulkarni, as well as students from CSCI-4020 Computer Algorithms in the spring of 2002 and 2003, David R. Musser is currently developing a collection of algorithm concept descriptions called Algorithm Concepts. This document contains Section 1 of the book.

Basic Algorithm Concepts

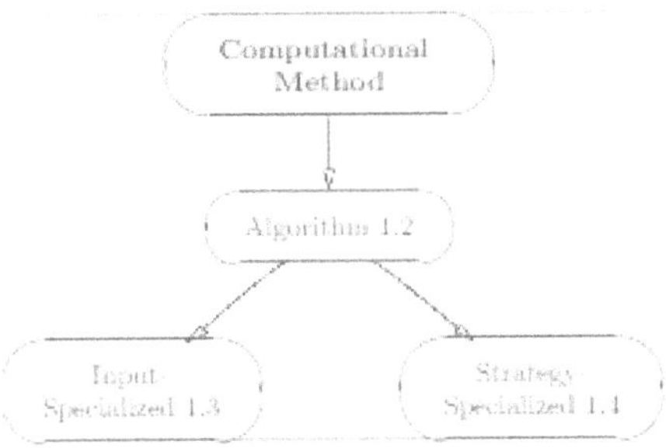

Source: - (Upadhyay, 2024)

An algorithm is a way to solve a specific type of problem using a finite set of stages. These steps take inputs, which are quantities given to the algorithm either before or during execution, and produce one or more outputs that are related to the inputs in some way. In addition to being finite, the method's step count must be independent of the inputs. (The program's size is unrelated to the inputs, albeit it may exhibit distinct variants for various input types.) The method must also adhere to resource constraints, which limit the amount of time and space that can be utilised for method executions. These constraints apply to all operations within the method's phases.

Algorithm

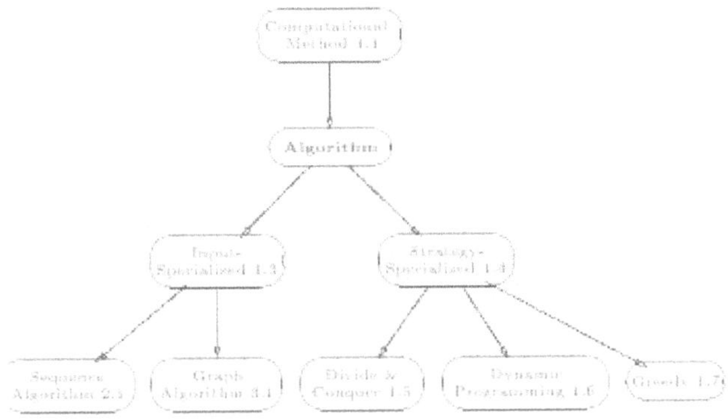

Source: - (Upadhyay, 2024)

Refinement of: Section 1.1: Computational Method computing technique is considered finite if and only if there is a finite number of steps in each execution of the method. The method is said to be ending when it exhibits the fininess quality, which is also known as termination. A computational technique (§1.1) with the extra property of finiteness is often known as an algorithm, which is a synonym for finite computational method. The termination characteristic is an essential feature of every algorithmic abstraction.

Algorithm Specialized by Input

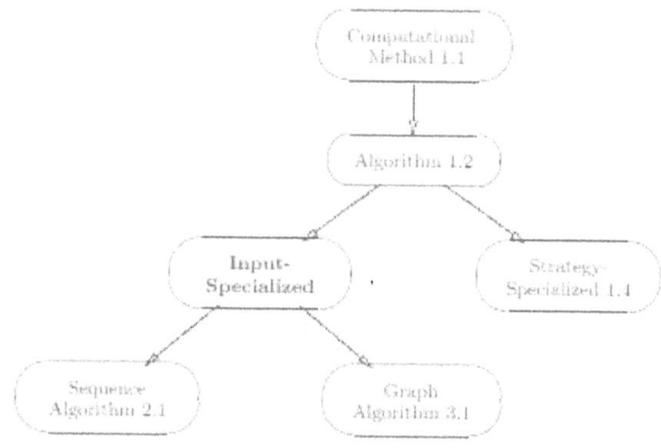

Source: - (Upadhyay, 2024)

By imposing limitations on the input format, this idea condenses the algorithm (§1.2) concept. Sets, graphs, or linear sequences are just a few examples of the domains that subconcepts limit their input to.

Algorithm Specialized by Strategy

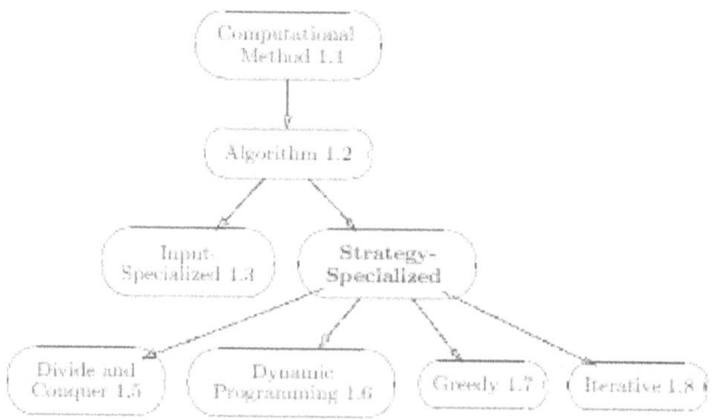

Source: - (Upadhyay, 2024)

In terms of strategies employed to structure the stages of the algorithm, this idea is a reduction of the algorithm (§1.2) concept. The following algorithms have been refined: Divide-and-Conquer (§1.5), Dynamic Programming (§1.6), Greedy (§1.7), and Iterative (§1.8).5

8.2. Milestones in Evolutionary Computation

<u>**Evolutionary Milestones**</u>

Documenting and understanding key transitions in the evolution of life on Earth.

In the course of human existence, there are defining moments. For instance, following abiogenesis and the emergence of the first living things, eukaryotic cells (those containing a nucleus) emerged during early evolution. The first ecological interactions between different species also began around this time, as did the chain reaction that led to the development of eukaryotic cells with mitochondria and other organelles.

Sometime after 1 billion years ago, several creatures evolved into multicellular ones; animals began to incorporate hard pieces into their body plans (and diversified quickly); and land-dwelling plants and animals eventually became part of the unicellular kingdom. We may examine these occurrences in great detail by consulting the fossil record. The dates of important nodes in the evolutionary tree, the relationships between life and its environment across geological time, and the origins of evolutionary breakthroughs can all be better understood with this information.

Our current work on such milestones includes studies on:

- The organic geochemistry of ancient bacterial mats
- The earliest unicellular organisms that lived on land and their ecological interactions
- The earliest biomineralising animals
- The nature of the Cambrian explosion

- Early land animals, including the origins and early evolution of insects and arachnids.

Computer modelling of evolution over palaeontological timescales is one area that will be further explored in future research, along with other emerging approaches for extracting additional data from fossil records.

Types of Evolutionary Algorithms

What are Evolutionary Algorithms?

Computational models that draw inspiration from Charles Darwin's theory of natural evolution are known as Evolutionary Algorithms (EAs). By mimicking natural selection, mutation, recombination, and competition, they help optimise many different types of issues. The use of EAs has grown in fields such as biology, engineering, economics, and artificial intelligence since its inception in the 1960s.

Functionality and Features: A fitness function, genetic operators, a selection process, and a population of solutions are the four primary parts of an EA. Iteratively utilising selection, crossover, and mutation, the algorithm builds an initial population at random, assesses the fitness of each individual, and optimises the solutions.

Benefits and Use Cases: EAs offer several advantages over traditional optimization techniques, including flexibility, robustness, and the ability to handle complex, multi-modal, and noisy problem domains. They are particularly beneficial in domains where the exact solution is hard to obtain. EAs are used in various applications such as feature selection, pathfinder algorithm in games, and machine learning.

Challenges and Limitations: While highly versatile, EAs can be computationally expensive, especially for large-scale problems. They may also get stuck in local optima and require careful parameter tuning. Additionally, EAs may not be suitable for all types of problems, specifically those with a limited solution space.

Integration with Data Lakehouse: Evolutionary Algorithms can play a crucial role in a Data Lakehouse environment, primarily by assisting in data management and optimization tasks. Data scientists can utilize EAs to refine and optimize complex queries, extract patterns, and manage data quality within the Data Lakehouse. Moreover, EAs can complement the analytical capabilities of a Data Lakehouse, providing rich insights and predictions.

Security Aspects: While EAs themselves do not incorporate any specific security features, the application of EAs should be aligned with the overall security protocol of the system they are integrated into. In a Data Lakehouse environment, this includes adhering to data governance and access control policies.

Performance: The performance of EAs is heavily dependent on the system configuration and the quality of parameter tuning. Well-configured EAs can offer high-quality solutions and significantly boost analytical performance in a Data Lakehouse setup.

9. *Genetic Algorithms*

<u>Introduction to Optimization</u>

Improving something by making it better is what optimisation is all about. As seen in the image below, every process has inputs and outputs.

Source: - (Tutorialspoint, 2024)

The goal of optimisation is to identify the set of inputs that, when combined, produce the "best" score. In mathematics, "best" typically refers to determining the input parameters with the maximum or minimum value that maximise or minimise some objective function, though this definition might vary depending on the task at hand.

The space of potential solutions or values that the inputs can take is called the search space. The ideal answer is located at some point in this search space. Locating that point (or points) in the search space is the goal of optimisation.

What are Genetic Algorithms?

Over the ages, people have found a tremendous deal of motivation and wisdom in nature. Search algorithms that draw from genetics and natural selection are known as genetic algorithms (GAs). Among the several subfields that make up Evolutionary Computation, GAs are one of the most prominent.

A number of optimisation problems have been successfully tackled using GAs, which were created by John Holland and his colleagues and students at the University of Michigan, with special mention to David E. Goldberg.

With GAs, we start with a population of potential answers to the topic at hand. Similar to natural genetics, these solutions are recombinant and mutated to create new offspring, and this cycle continues for many generations. Each potential solution or individual's fitness level is defined by the value of the goal function. To increase the number of "fitter" individuals, the best individuals are given more opportunities to marry. Charles Darwin's "Survival of the Fittest" theory is consistent with this.

Generation after generation, we keep "evolving" into better versions of ourselves or our problems until something stops us.

To surpass random local search—in which we merely attempt many random solutions and record the best so far—genetic algorithms incorporate historical data in addition to their appropriately random nature.

Advantages of GAs

GAs have various advantages which have made them immensely popular. These include

- Does not require any derivative information (which may not be available for many real-world problems).

- Is faster and more efficient as compared to the traditional methods.

- Has very good parallel capabilities.

- Optimizes both continuous and discrete functions and also multi-objective problems.

- Provides a list of "good" solutions and not just a single solution.

- Always gets an answer to the problem, which gets better over the time.

- Useful when the search space is very large and there are a large number of parameters involved.

Limitations of GAs

- Like any technique, GAs also suffer from a few limitations. These include –

- GAs are not suited for all problems, especially problems which are simple and for which derivative information is available.

- Fitness value is calculated repeatedly which might be computationally expensive for some problems.

- Being stochastic, there are no guarantees on the optimality or the quality of the solution.

- If not implemented properly, the GA may not converge to the optimal solution.

9.1. Basic Principles

Maintaining due process is an important function of the legal system. For instance, solicitors safeguard their clients' entitlement to a just trial. A future where lawyers can practise freely and independently is a goal that Lawyers for Lawyers is striving to achieve. According to the United Nations Basic Principles on the Role of Lawyers, this is our primary objective.

What are the Basic Principles?

To ensure that everyone has access to impartial legal representation, the Basic Principles on the Role of Lawyers outline the essential needs. For instance, as stated in the Basic Principles, everyone is entitled to seek the advice of an impartial lawyer whenever they so desire. However, they do state that solicitors have the right to do their jobs well and according to established ethical guidelines.

The Basic Principles specify both lawyers' and governments' rights and duties to ensure a fair trial, including governments' duties to ensure that:

- lawyers are able to perform all of their professional functions without intimidation, hindrance, harassment or improper interference;

- lawyers have access to the information, files and documents required to provide their clients with effective legal assistance;

- there is no discrimination based on grounds like race, sex, religion or political preference with respect to the possibility to become a lawyer;

- lawyers are not identified with their clients as a result of discharging their functions;

- communications between lawyers and clients are recognized as confidential.

Broad support

- The Basic Principles were adopted by the United Nations General Assembly on September 30, 1990. The Basic Principles are more of a "soft-law" instrument than a piece of "hard law," meaning they cannot be forced upon anyone. Conversely, the Basic Principles are universally respected and agreed upon. The UN, other NGOs, and (regional) courts of justice all make use of the Basic Principles as an example. Some have even gone as far as to claim that the Basic Principles constitute a source of material law or that they mirror international customary law. The following rights are also included in regional and international human rights accords that are legally enforceable:

- International Covenant on Civil and Political Rights;

- Convention Against Torture and Other Cruel, Inhumane or Degrading Treatment and Punishment;

- International Covenant on Economic, Social and Cultural Rights;

- European Convention on Human Rights;

- American Convention on Human Rights;

- African Charter on Human and Peoples' Rights

9.2. Variants and Extensions

Evolutionary computation (EC) is a broad field of artificial intelligence that draws inspiration from biological evolution to solve complex optimization problems. Over time, various variants and extensions of evolutionary algorithms (EAs) have been developed to improve performance, adaptability, and applicability across different problem domains. Below is an overview of the main EC variants and their key extensions.

1. Genetic Algorithms (GA)

Concept: Inspired by Darwinian evolution, GAs use crossover, mutation, and selection to evolve a population of solutions over generations.

Variants:

- **Binary-coded GAs:** Solutions are represented as binary strings.

- **Real-coded GAs:** Solutions are represented as real-valued vectors.

- **Steady-state GA:** Only a small portion of the population is replaced at each generation.

- **Multi-objective GA:** Optimizes multiple conflicting objectives (e.g., NSGA-II).

Extensions:

- **Adaptive GAs:** Adaptive mechanisms adjust crossover/ mutation rates dynamically.

- **Hybrid GAs:** Combine GAs with other optimization techniques like local search (memetic algorithms).

2. Genetic Programming (GP)

Concept: Evolve computer programs (typically represented as trees) instead of fixed-length strings or vectors.

Variants:

- **Strongly-typed GP:** Enforces data-type constraints to ensure syntactically correct programs.

- **Cartesian GP:** Represents programs as directed graphs rather than trees.

Extensions:

- **Pareto GP:** Handles multi-objective problems.

- **Linear GP:** Programs are represented as sequences of instructions.

3. Evolution Strategies (ES)

Concept: Focuses on evolving real-valued vectors, using self-adaptive mutation rates to explore the search space.

Variants:

- **(μ + λ) ES:** Selects the next generation from both parents and offspring.

- **(μ, λ) ES:** Selects the next generation only from offspring.

Extensions:

- **Covariance Matrix Adaptation ES (CMA-ES):** An advanced ES where the covariance matrix of mutations is adapted during evolution, enabling efficient exploration of complex search spaces.

4. Differential Evolution (DE)

Concept: A population-based optimization algorithm focused on evolving real-valued vectors, using a strategy of "mutation" and "crossover" specific to vector differences.

Variants:

- **DE/rand/1/bin:** The most common variant where a random individual is chosen for mutation.

- **DE/best/1/bin:** The best individual is used for mutation.

- **Multi-objective DE:** Optimizes multiple objectives.

Extensions:

- **Adaptive DE (JADE):** Adapts the control parameters like crossover rate dynamically.

- **Constrained DE:** Designed for constrained optimization problems.

5. **Particle Swarm Optimization (PSO)**

Concept: Inspired by social behavior, particles move through the search space, updating their positions based on individual and global best solutions.

Variants:

- **Standard PSO:** Basic version where particles update positions and velocities.

- **Multi-objective PSO:** Optimizes multiple conflicting objectives.

- **Binary PSO:** Discrete version of PSO for binary-valued problems.

Extensions:

- **Quantum-behaved PSO (QPSO):** Introduces quantum mechanics principles into particle behavior.

- Adaptive PSO: Modifies inertia and other parameters based on swarm behavior during the search.

10. *Genetic Programming*

To achieve the best possible outcome, genetic programming uses an AI method that is based on natural selection. In genetic programming, the algorithm iteratively selects the most advantageous "offspring" (often called a fitness function) to breed with in subsequent generations. Similar to how organisms undergo random mutations during evolution, evolutionary algorithms can also produce genetically improved children. However, as only the fittest individuals are passed down through the generations, fitness steadily rises. When a genetic program achieves a certain level of fitness, it will typically stop. Furthermore, existing programs can have architecture-altering procedures added to them to enable the analysis of additional sources of data for a certain fitness function.

Genetic algorithms weren't successfully applied until the 1980s, even though Alan Turing first suggested them in 1950. Bioinformatics pioneer John Koza patented the first algorithm for genetic operations in 1988. Annual conferences like Genetic Algorithms and specialised magazines like Genetic Programming and Evolvable Machines reflect the growing body of literature around genetic operations as a field of study. Additionally, Genetic and Evolutionary Computation is a collection of nineteen works published by MIT Press. There is now a larger pool of computer programs capable of running evolutionary programs due to the growth in our understanding of these programs.

Automatic programming, involving no human intervention, is one feature of genetic programming systems, which employ a machine learning technique. In other words, as more data is fed into genetic algorithms, they can automatically optimise their programs by doing program inductions. When an exact answer is unknown or when an approximation is acceptable, genetic or evolutionary algorithms can be useful. These algorithms find use in many disciplines. Because of its use in carrying out symbolic regressions and feature classifications, genetic programming is frequently employed with other types of machine learning.

Genetic programming can help organizations and businesses by:

- **Saving time:** When compared to humans, genetic algorithms significantly outperform them when it comes to processing massive data sets. Also, these algorithms don't have any inherent biases that humans do, thus they can generate ideas that would have been overlooked before.

- **Data and text classification:** There is no longer any requirement for human intervention in the data classification and identification processes thanks to genetic programming. Data tree construction is a tool that genetic programming can employ to enhance these classifications, particularly when working with large datasets.

- **Ensuring network security:** New network assaults have been identified using rule evolution methodologies. Organisations and corporations can protect sensitive data from intrusions if they can detect them in a timely manner and respond accordingly.

- **Supporting other machine learning methods:** Neural networks and other bigger machine learning systems can use genetic programming. Organisations can speed up the processing of data for integration into larger or other learning methods by directing genetic programming to focus on certain groups of data. Organisations can collect as much valuable and practical data as possible in this way.

10.1. Representation of Programs

It has already been stated that memory stores not just data but also the program to be executed as an ordered list of instructions. Figure 1.1 depicts the central processing unit (CPU), which is in charge of retrieving instructions from memory and carrying out the data operation as instructed. In Figure 1.3, we can see the central processing unit (CPU) and its memory in greater depth. The ALU, Registers, and Control Unit are three essential parts of the central processing unit (CPU).

Digital circuits called "Arithmetic Logic Units" (ALUs) may do logic operations (AND, OR) and arithmetic (add, subtract) on data. For short-term data storage, the central processing unit (CPU) uses registers, which are like a little scratchpad memory. In order to direct all operations within the machine, an additional circuit called the Control Unit analyses instructions to identify which operation to perform and then controls the other circuits to carry it out.

Mathematical and logic operations (AND, OR) and data addition and subtraction are both performed by digital circuits known as "Arithmetic Logic Units" (ALUs). The central processing unit (CPU) makes use of registers, which are analogous to small scratchpad memory, to temporarily store data. An extra circuit known as the Control Unit examines instructions to determine which action to do, and then it controls the other circuits to carry it out, in order to direct all machine processes.

What follows is an explanation of the binary coding scheme that the computer uses to store programs. Here we will go over what is known as the computer's machine language, an encoding of this kind.

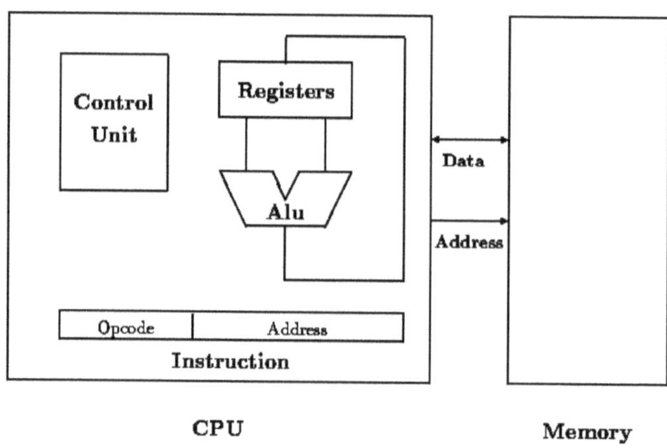

Figure 1.3: CPU and Memory Configuration

Source: - (Oreilly, 2024)

<u>Machine Language</u>

The instruction set is a collection of basic operations that a computer's central processing unit (CPU) may execute. These actions are often relatively simple. This set contains instructions that can load data from one location to another, like as from memory to a CPU register. In a similar vein, there are instructions to store data in memory rather than the CPU. Furthermore, there are directives for performing mathematical operations, such add, on values of data. There are other instructions that regulate the program's execution;

specifically, they specify the location in memory from which the following instruction should be retrieved. Although control instructions typically fetch instructions in a sequential fashion, with the next instruction being retrieved from the address in memory after this one, they can test a condition and dictate that the next instruction be retrieved from a different location in memory instead. Lastly, the set might include contain commands for "housekeeping" tasks performed by the system, such managing external I/O devices.

Some standard for describing the meaning of the instruction's bits is required in order to encode them in binary form for memory storage. A data item's address and an identifier for the instruction itself (the opcode or operation code) are the two most common pieces of information needed to carry out the majority of the aforementioned tasks. In Figure 1.3, in the instruction block, you can see these components.

Machine language refers to a set of instructions coded in binary form, while program refers to the collection of these instructions. Writing or understanding such a program is quite challenging. Imagine for a second a world where all your thoughts are based on binary codes for extremely basic commands and on binary memory addresses for data items. This isn't something you should do unless your software is really small. Advanced programming languages better suit human intelligence and communication styles are necessary. Consequently, there is a programming language called assembly language that is somewhat higher up the stack than machine language and is extremely similar to machine language. There is one machine language instruction for every assembly instruction. Having names instead of binary representations for the instructions and memory cells is the biggest benefit. Data addresses and operational codes (sometimes known as mnemonics or names for instructions to help with memory) are both included in assembly instructions. Figure 1.4 shows a very basic code fragment for the machine mentioned before. Both the machine code and its assembly language counterparts are displayed in the figure. Memory cell definitions are provided below the code snippet.

```
Program Fragment:        Y = Y + X

Machine Language Code                        Assembly Language
(Binary Code)                                     Code

Opcode           Address
1100 0000        0010 0000 0000 0000              LOAD  Y
1011 0000        0001 0000 0000 0000              ADD   X
1001 0000        0010 0000 0000 0000              STORE Y


Memory Cell Definitions:

    Addr.       Name       Cell Contents

    1000        X          32
    2000        Y          16
```

Figure 1.4: Machine and Assembly Language Program Fragment

Source: - (Oreilly, 2024)

In binary format, the machine language code is displayed. Every instruction has its own unique address, which is 16 bits long, and an opcode that is 8 bits long. The assembly language code provides a slightly clearer view of the program's functionality. ''Y'' is the address in memory that the first instruction loads into the CPU register, which is sometimes referred to as the accumulator for CPUs with a single register. Adding the data from address ''X'' in memory to the data in the accumulator and then storing the sum back in the accumulator is the second instruction. The last step is to return the accumulator's value to memory at address ''Y''. Based on the data values displayed in the graphic, the position referred to as "Y" at the end of this program fragment will have the value 48.

We propose a utility application that can convert assembly language code that humans can read into machine language code that a central processing unit (CPU) can understand. The name of this application is the assembler. The source program is the original code written in assembly language or another higher-level language; the object program is the code that is assembled into machine language. Programs' source and object codes are also known as "code" and "code."

Even though assembly language is a huge leap forward from machine language, we are still limited to performing repetitive and error-prone operations on data using relatively basic operations like load, store, add, etc. Luckily, translators (called compilers) have been developed to transform lower-level programming languages to higher-level languages that are more closely aligned with our way of thinking about programming. The language C is one example; it is presented in Section 2 and is the focus of this article.

10.2. Applications and Challenges

The term "real-time" is gaining popularity, but what exactly does it imply? Time is of the essence in real-time applications. While the exact amount of time that a "real-time" application must display is not defined by any particular standard, it is reasonable to assume that the user will not be able to see that the software is processing data in real-time. To rephrase, it should be considered an immediate answer.

Forecasts made by IDC indicate that by 2025, 30% of the world's data will be in real-time. The complex ecology in which data sources exist, along with their ever-growing and changing nature, presents organisations with a formidable challenge. For some sectors, this is of paramount importance. As an example, real-time retail is ranked in the top three goals for 44% of retailers.

Traditional Streaming Solutions

Traditional data streaming systems provide methods to help standardise and integrate different data sources. However, the protocols upon which these technologies are built, such as REST and SOAP, rely on polling, and these cannot meet the needs of processing data in real-time. In today's intricate digital ecosystems, architectures might combine polling-based, event-based, and custom infrastructures, each with its own unique set of integration requirements.

Disruptions and other inefficiencies are brought about by every merger. Applications that are hard to scale and have little flexibility are the result of all these integrations. The objectives of a real-time application are inherently at odds with the construction of a complicated system of loosely connected components.

The Benefits of an Intelligent Data Mesh

By acting as a central repository for all of an organization's data and offering intelligence at the network's periphery, an Intelligent Data Mesh may optimise, disseminate, and manage real-time data from any source. Any industry that can benefit from the rapid dissemination of data has a use case: geo-location data, streams from Internet of Things sensors, sports and trade channels, and countless more.

The most modern solutions integrate real-time capabilities with the benefits of classic streaming tools. To create a consolidated system for handling and disseminating real-time data, they integrate polling and event-based back-ends.

The Issue of Scalability

Developing and releasing new application programming interfaces (APIs) can feel like an endless chore when there is so much data to consolidate and link. There are ramifications for more than just the people directly involved with customers; internal stakeholders and business partners also have frequent interactions with data and apps.

Scalability is a major challenge for software architects and developers working on real-time applications. As your user base expands, scalability means keeping up the same level of reliability and performance. When faced with a scalability problem, it is not sufficient to just throw hardware at it.

Solving the Scalability Challenge

Intelligent data meshes are valuable because of their capacity to manage real-time data and how well the solution deals with distribution size. Various forms of scalability are necessary for the many business applications. These include supporting high data throughput across geographically scattered or remote regions, handling tens or hundreds of thousands of distinct data streams, and accommodating enormous and frequently fluctuating client volumes. The operational difficulty of synchronising data and monitoring systems, together with the huge number of server instances needed to sustain heavy traffic loads, is a common complaint about REST-based techniques.

Let's Not Forget Security

Security naturally takes centre stage when APIs must be accessible to a large number of users. When it comes to transporting data, access control is paramount for every firm. If not handled properly, exposing data feeds in real-time might increase operational risk. Concurrently, there is a huge potential for income development thanks to the capacity to disclose real-time feeds.

To provide centralised security control over real-time data, an Intelligent Data Mesh can function as a single access point. With the help of a pluggable authentication system, companies can implement identity control across all data using SSO, LDAP, or custom authentication, and they can also take advantage of dynamic authorisation and fine-grained permissions for granular access control, making it easy to grant or revoke privileges as needed (Hughes, 2020).

Web, mobile, and Internet of Things (IoT) applications that run in real-time can be difficult for developers and software architects to create. Managerial and integration challenges spanning back-end and front-end codebases are a common occurrence for them. The majority of programmers are proficient at building reliable back-end systems. Unfortunately, there aren't many possibilities for tools and development gets considerably more complicated when data has to be pushed out into other contexts, sometimes across crowded or unstable networks like the web, mobile, or satellite networks. At this point, an Intelligent Data Mesh becomes crucial.

11. Evolution Strategies

This article will teach you how to train a neural network in Python using Evolution Strategies (ES) without back-propagation. You will use the MNIST Handwritten Digit dataset as your starting point. The idea can be further understood and applied to other appropriate contexts with the help of this modest implementation. Alright, let's begin!

a. Numerical Optimization

Almost every machine learning method can be effectively framed as an optimisation problem. By adjusting the parameters of the model, a machine learning algorithm seeks to reduce loss. One way to express any supervised learning algorithm is as $\theta\_estimate = argmin\ \mathbb{E}[L(y,f(x,\theta))]$. The features are represented by x and the target by y. The model parameters are denoted by θ. The function we are attempting to model is denoted by f. The Loss function, which calculates the quality of our fit, is represented by L. Typically, these kinds of issues are well-solved using the Gradient Descent algorithm, which is also called steepest descent. It uses a first-order iterative technique to find the local minimum of a differentiable function. We are doing steps at each current position that are directly proportional to the negative gradient of the Loss function, denoted as $\theta\_new = \theta\_old - \alpha * \nabla L(y, f(x, \theta\_old))$. The Newton's approach is another iterative method that converges with fewer iterations. However, it is second-order and computationally intensive because it needs to calculate the inverse of the second-order derivative of the loss function (the Hessian matrix), $\theta\_new = \theta\_old - [\nabla^2 L(y, f(x, \theta\_old))]$. This is represented as $^{(-1)} * \nabla L(y, f(x, \theta\_old))$. Using gradients to determine a parameter is our expectation for discovering a loss-reducing strategy. Can we, however, find the best parameters without using gradient calculations? Actually, I can think of a lot of ways to fix this! Various derivitive-free optimisation strategies, sometimes called black-box optimisation, are available.

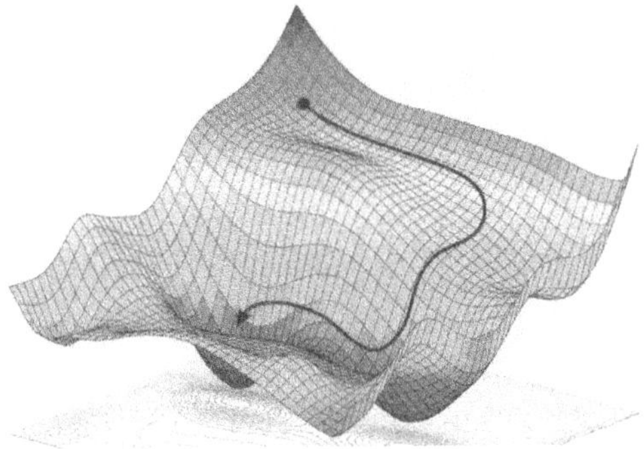

Source: - (Jin et al., 2024)

b. **Evolution Strategies**

It is possible that gradient descent won't work every time. Why? Short and sweet, the answer is local optimal. Consider a chess game where the final score is +1 or -1 for a victory or loss, respectively, as an example of a sparse reward scenario in reinforcement learning. The agent receives this reward at the end of the episode. If we don't win, we'll have no idea if we were completely off our game or if it was just a fluke. We can become stuck since the reward gradient signal is mostly useless. Evolution Strategies (ES) and other derivative-free methods are preferable to noisy gradients for updating parameters. When this occurs, or when we are unable to directly calculate the gradients or when we do not know the exact analytic form of the objective function, ES is a good choice.

c. **Vanilla Implementation**

Parameters are initially generated at random and then fine-tuned until they achieve slightly higher performance. To generate a population of, say, one hundred slightly different parameter vectors θ_1, $\theta_2...\theta_{100}$, in mathematics, we employ Gaussian noise to jitter a parameter vector θ at each step. After that, we evaluate the 100 candidates' performance by running the model on their own and looking at the output result. Because of this, we can find out whether the loss or objective function worked. Our next best parameter will be the mean of the top N performing elite parameters (where N might be as high as 10). Next, we derive 100 additional parameters by combining the best one thus far with some Gaussian noise.

Natural selection theory suggests that we should view this as a process of selecting the most effective parameters from a pool of potential ones, after which we can use this selection to inform our decision-making. We then use a really simplistic approach—taking the mean of all these parameters—but it works! This yields what we call our optimal parameter. Once convergence is achieved, we repopulate the population by adding random noise to this parameter.

Not all giraffes have equally long necks. Giraffes inherit their neck length from their parents. It is largely fixed by genes.

Food that are easily accessed will be eaten by many animal species, and is therefore easily gone. If this happens, giraffes with longer neck are more likely to survive. They can reach food that few other can reach.

Over time, more and more of the giraffes came to have long necks (the short ones never made it to reproduction). This is what we call natural selection and evoluationary adapation.

Source: - (Biswas, 2020)

1. Pseudo Code:

Randomly initialize the best parameter using a Gaussian distribution

2. Loop until convergence:

- Create population of parameters $\theta_1, \theta_2 ... \theta_{100}$ by adding Gaussian noise to the best parameter

- Evaluate the objective function for all the parameters and select the top N best performing parameters (elite parameters)

- Best parameter = Mean (top N elite parameters)

- Decay the noise at the end of each iteration by some factor (At the start more noise will help us to explore better but as we reach the convergence point we want the noise to be minimum so as to not deviate away)

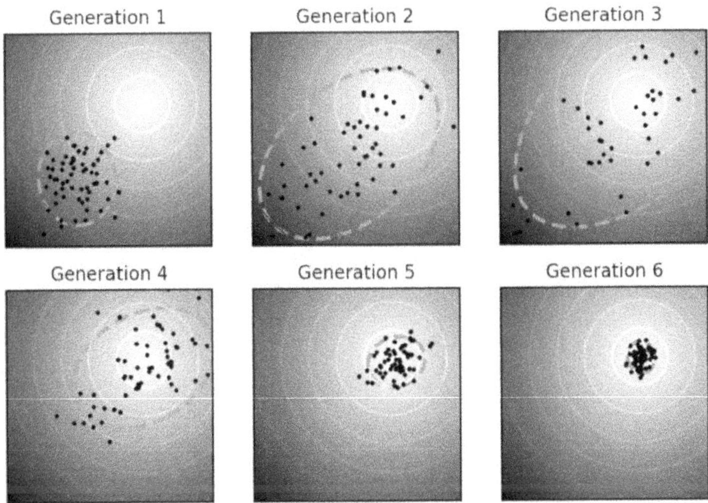

Source: - (Biswas, 2020)

d. Python Implementation from scratch

To help you understand, I'll walk you through a basic Python example. For a couple of the items, I also attempted to include details pertaining to numerical stability. Take a look at the feedback! The MNIST Handwritten Digit dataset and the necessary libraries will be loaded first.

e. Ending note

ES are very simple to implement and don't require gradients. Just by injecting noise into our parameters we are able to search the parameter space. Even though we have solved it for a supervised problem for the ease of understanding, it is more suited for Reinforcement learning scenarios where one has to estimate the gradient of the expected reward by sampling.

11.1. Mutation Operators

GA is the mutation operator, which works on the level of chromosome genes by randomly altering a gene value. Mutation introduces innovation into the population by randomly modifying the chromosomes. The operation is designed to prevent GA from premature termination since it prevents the population from becoming saturated with chromosomes that look alike. Usually considered as a background operator, the role of the mutation operator is often seen as guaranteeing that the probability of searching any given chromosome will never be zero. In GAs, mutation is randomly applied with low probability and modifies chromosome elements. Large mutation rates increase the likelihood of destroying good chromosomes but prevent premature convergence. The mutation rate determines the probability that mutation will occur.

The mutation operator maintains the stochastic nature of the algorithm by maintaining the genetic diversity of the current generation to the next one. The mutation operator provides chances for candidate solutions that cannot be obtained only by using the crossover operator application in the binary format. This operator randomly manipulates the chromosome with a specific rate called mutation rate (β), for the continuously coded chromosomes.

In this section, we describe some of the most commonly used mutation operators. Like the crossover operators, this is not an exhaustive list and the GA designer might find a combination of these approaches or a problem-specific mutation operator more useful.

Bit-flip Mutation

Bit flip mutation is a fundamental operator that introduces diversity and enables exploration of the search space. This section will dive into the details of bit flip mutation, its probability, and how it balances exploration and exploitation.

What is Bit Flip Mutation

Bit flip mutation is a simple yet effective operator that modifies individual solutions represented as bitstrings. In this process, each bit in the bitstring has a chance to be flipped, i.e., changing a 0 to a 1 or vice versa. For example, given a bitstring 1001, a bit flip mutation might result in 1011, where the third bit has been flipped.

The bit flip mutation operator is crucial in genetic algorithms as it helps maintain genetic diversity within the population. By randomly modifying bits, it allows the algorithm to explore new regions of the search space and potentially discover better solutions.

Probability of Mutation Operator

The probability of mutation determines the likelihood of each bit being flipped during the mutation process. A higher mutation probability results in more bits being flipped on average, while a lower probability leads to fewer changes.

Choosing the right mutation probability is a balancing act. A high mutation probability promotes exploration by introducing more diversity, but it may also disrupt good solutions. Conversely, a low mutation probability focuses on exploiting existing solutions, but it may cause the algorithm to stagnate.

Common Values and Their Impact

Typically, mutation probabilities range from 0.001 to 0.1, with a common rule of thumb being to set the mutation probability inversely proportional to the population size. For instance, if the population size is 100, a mutation probability of 0.01 might be appropriate.

Here is a list of common bit flip mutation rates, including specific values and heuristics:

1. **Fixed mutation rates**

   - 1/L (where L is the length of the bitstring)

     o Often used as a default value

     o Provides a balance between exploration and exploitation

   - (1%)

     o A low mutation rate that favors exploitation over exploration

     o Suitable for problems with a smooth fitness landscape

   - 0.05 (5%)

     o A moderate mutation rate that balances exploration and exploitation

     o Applicable to a wide range of problems

- (10%)
    - A high mutation rate that emphasizes exploration
    - Useful for problems with a rugged fitness landscape or when the population diversity is low

2. **Adaptive mutation rates:**

- Decrease mutation rate over time
    - Start with a high mutation rate (e.g., 0.1) and gradually decrease it as the algorithm progresses
    - Encourages exploration in the early stages and exploitation in the later stages
- Increase mutation rate when the population diversity is low
    - Monitor the population diversity (e.g., using Hamming distance) and increase the mutation rate when diversity falls below a threshold
    - Helps prevent premature convergence and stagnation

3. **Heuristics for setting mutation rates**

- Rule of thumb: $1/L$ (where L is the length of the bitstring)
    - A simple and effective heuristic that provides a good starting point
- Mutation rate should be inversely proportional to the population size
    - Smaller populations benefit from higher mutation rates to maintain diversity
    - Larger populations can afford lower mutation rates as they inherently have more diversity
- Optimal mutation rate depends on the problem and the stage of the algorithm
    - Experiment with different mutation rates and adapt them based on the problem characteristics and the algorithm's performance

11.2. Covariance Matrix Adaptation

The covariance matrix adaptation evolution strategy (CMA-ES) is one of the most powerful evolutionary algorithms for real-valued single-objective optimization. In this paper, we develop a variant of the CMA-ES for multi-objective optimization (MOO). We first introduce a single-objective, elitist CMA-ES using plus-selection and step size control based on a success rule. This algorithm is compared to the standard CMA-ES. The elitist CMA-ES turns out to be slightly faster on unimodal functions, but is more prone to getting stuck in sub-optimal local minima. In the new multi-objective CMAES (MO-CMA-ES) a population of individuals that adapt their search strategy as in the elitist CMA-ES is maintained. These are subject to multi-objective selection. The selection is based on non-dominated sorting using either the crowding-distance or the contributing hypervolume as second sorting criterion. Both the elitist single-objective CMA-ES and the MO-CMA-ES inherit important invariance properties, in particular invariance against rotation of the search space, from the original CMA-ES. The benefits of the new MO-CMA-ES in comparison to the well-known NSGA-II and to NSDE, a multi-objective differential evolution algorithm, are experimentally shown.

The CMA-ES does not require a tedious parameter tuning for its application. In fact, the choice of strategy internal parameters is not left to the user (arguably with the exception of population size λ). Finding good (default) strategy parameters is considered as part of the algorithm design, and not part of its application—the aim is to have a well-performing algorithm as is. The default population size λ is comparatively small to allow for fast convergence. Restarts with increasing population size improve the global search performance. For the application of the CMA-ES, an initial solution, an initial standard deviation (step-size, variables should be defined such that the same standard deviations can be reasonably applied to all variables) and, possibly, the termination criteria (e.g. a function tolerance) need to be set by the user. The most common applications are model calibration (e.g. curve fitting) and shape optimisation.

The heatmap below shows the values of this function — brighter colors mean a higher value. The function has the global minimum in the origin $(0, 0)$, but it's peppered with many local extremes. We need to find the global minimum via CMA-ES.

Source: - (Andrei, 2024)

CMA-ES is based on the multivariate normal distribution. It generates test points in the search space from this distribution. You will have to guess the original mean value of the distribution, and its standard deviation, but after that the algorithm will iteratively modify all these parameters, sweeping the distribution through the search space, looking for the best objective function values. Here's the original distribution that the test points are drawn from:

A population of 6 points was generated in the image above, which is the default population size picked by the optimizer for this problem. This is the first step. After this, the algorithm needs to:

- compute the objective function (Rastrigin) for each point

- update the mean, the standard deviation, and the covariance matrix, effectively creating a new multivariate normal distribution, based on what it has learned from the objective function

- generate a new set of test points from the new distribution

- repeat until some criterion is fulfilled (either converge on some mean value, or exceed the maximum number of steps, etc.)

12. *Differential Evolution*

The use of differential evolution allows for the global heuristic optimisation of nonlinear and non-differentiable continuous space functions.

A computer's differential evolution algorithm is just one member of a much bigger family of evolutionary algorithms. Differential evolution algorithm, like other famous direct search methods, starts with a population of possible solutions, much like evolution strategies and genetic algorithms. Iteratively improving the population of fittest candidate solutions by adding mutations keeps them from producing a higher objective function value.

The differential evolution algorithm beats the other popular methods because it can handle nonlinear and non-differentiable multi-dimensional goal functions and because it uses sparse control parameters to minimise steering. Because of these improvements, the algorithm is now more accessible and useful.

Learn how to optimise your global strategy with the help of the differential evolution algorithm in this comprehensive guide.

After completing this tutorial, you will know:

- Differential evolution is a heuristic approach for the global optimisation of nonlinear and non- differentiable continuous space functions.

- How to implement the differential evolution algorithm from scratch in Python.

- How to apply the differential evolution algorithm to a real-valued 2D objective function.

Tutorial Overview

This tutorial is divided into three parts; they are:

- Differential Evolution

- Differential Evolution Algorithm From Scratch

- Differential Evolution Algorithm on the Sphere Function

Differential Evolution

Differential evolution is a heuristic approach for the global optimisation of nonlinear and non- differentiable continuous space functions.

- For a minimisation algorithm to be considered practical, it is expected to fulfil five different requirements:

- Ability to handle non-differentiable, nonlinear and multimodal cost functions.

- Parallelizability to cope with computation intensive cost functions.

- Ease of use, i.e. few control variables to steer the minimization. These variables should

- also be robust and easy to choose.

- Good convergence properties, i.e. consistent convergence to the global minimum in

- consecutive independent trials.

12.1. Basic Mechanisms

Definitions: Link or Element, Pairing of Elements with degrees of freedom, Grubler's criterion (without derivation), Kinematic chain, Mechanism, Mobility of Mechanism, Inversions, Machine.

<u>Mechanisms:</u>

Quick return motion mechanisms – Drag link mechanism, Whitworth mechanism and Crank and slotted lever mechanism

- Straight line motion mechanisms – Peacelier's mechanism and Robert's mechanism.

- Intermittent motion mechanisms – Geneva mechanism and Ratchet & Pawl mechanism.

- Toggle mechanism, Pantograph, Hooke's joint and Ackerman Steering gear mechanism

Terminology and Definitions-Degree of Freedom, Mobility.

Kinematics: Analysis of motion (including location, speed, and acceleration). Acquiring the skill to create a system that meets defined motion requirements is a primary objective of learning kinematics. The focus of this course will be on this.

- **Kinetics:** The effect of forces on moving bodies. Good kinematic design should produce good kinetics.

- **Mechanism:** A system design to transmit motion. (low forces)

- **Machine:** A system designed to transmit motion and energy. (forces involved

- **Basic Mechanisms:** Includes geared systems, cam-follower systems and linkages (rigid links connected by sliding or rotating joints). A mechanism has multiple moving parts (for example, a simple hinged door does not qualify as a mechanism).

- **Examples of mechanisms:** Tin snips, vise grips, car suspension, backhoe, piston engine, folding chair, windshield wiper drive system, etc.

Key concepts:

- **Degrees of freedom:** The amount of data needed to fully manipulate a system. Consider a basic spinning link as an example. A system with two links. A connection with four bars. The five-bar connection.

- **Types of motion:** A mechanism can generate motions that are entirely translational, entirely rotational, or a hybrid of the two. In order to limit a mechanism's degrees of freedom, we can make it move only in certain directions, such as the x-y or z-axis in the case of a two-dimensional mechanism.

- **Link:** The ability to attach two or more stiff bodies together via a network of nodes, or joints. WM examples include binary links, ternary links with three joints, and quaternary links with four joints.

- **Joint:** The link that facilitates movement between the two other links. Joints that permit motion can be either revolute (allowing rotation), sliding (allowing translation), or a hybrid of the two (allowing roll-slide).

- **Kinematic chain:** A system of interconnected links and joints that allows two motions, one input and one output, to be coordinated.

- **Link or element:**

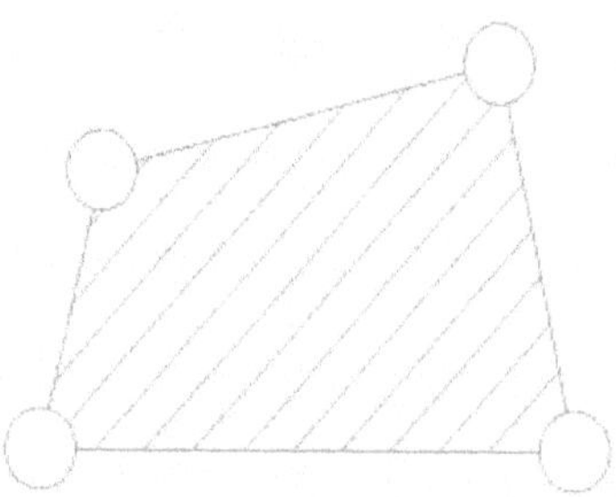

Source: - (BrainKart, 2023)

Many stiff bodies, some of which may move in relation to the others, make up a mechanism. A link is a set of rigidly connected resistive bodies that prevents them from moving relative to one another.

Another definition of a link is a part of a system that connects other parts and moves in relation to them; hence, a link could be made up of one or more resistant bodies. One other name for a link is an element or a kinematic link.

- **Kinematic Pair:**

When two links of a joint are in relative motion with one another, we call that a kinematic pair.

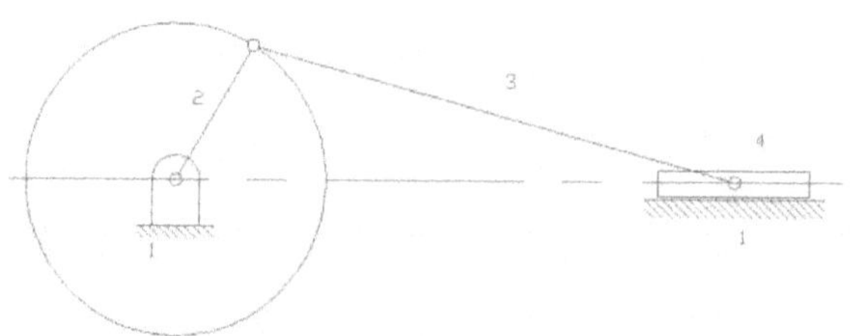

Source: - (BrainKart, 2023)

The second link in the Slider crank mechanism is a turning pair, or revolute, because it turns with respect to the first link. In a similar vein, turning pairs are formed by connections 2, 3, and 3, 4. This is a sliding pair, with link 4 (the slider) moving in the opposite direction of link 1.

12.2. Variants and Applications

Variants and applications are important ideas in many domains, including biology, technology, and machine learning. The term "variant" is frequently used in biology to describe a form of an organism or virus that has evolved through mutation. In genetics, for example, gene variants are caused by DNA sequence mutations, which might impact an individual's attributes or illness predisposition. In the context of infectious diseases, viral variations originate from changes in a virus's genomic code, potentially resulting in new strains, as was the case with SARS-CoV-2 during the COVID-19 pandemic. Understanding these variants is critical for creating targeted therapies, vaccinations, and diagnostic tests.

The term "variant" in machine learning can refer to different versions of a technique or model that have been optimised for specific applications. A neural network variant could, for example, be a convolutional neural network (CNN) for image recognition or an RNN for natural language processing applications. These model versions address various data sources and issue domains, enhancing the performance and application of ML approaches. Furthermore, these versions have applications in fields like healthcare, banking, and autonomous cars, where predicted accuracy and real-time decision-making are crucial.

<u>**Variants in Industrial Applications:**</u>

Variants are critical in industrial settings for manufacturing, supply chain optimisation, and product design. Manufacturing process variations, for example, may be created to accommodate varying production quantities, material limits, or regulatory norms. A variant of a production line may be introduced to handle high-end, low-volume production rather than mass production. Similarly, product versions are developed to target distinct market categories or geographical areas. To meet regional restrictions and consumer preferences, an automotive manufacturer may build variants of the same car model with differences in fuel type, safety features, or pollution standards.

<u>Applications in Industry:</u>

1. **Product Customization:** Developing product variants to cater to diverse customer preferences, such as cars with different features based on market needs.

2. **Manufacturing Processes:** Adapting production line variants for low-volume, high-customization versus high-volume, standardized products.

3. **Supply Chain Management:** Optimizing logistics and supply chains with variants that accommodate different regional regulations and market demands.

13. Chapter Summary

The chapter provides an overview of the historical development and key concepts in evolutionary computation (EC). It starts with the early algorithms and concepts that laid the foundation for EC, such as natural selection and survival of the fittest, which inspired the design of algorithms that mimic biological evolution. Milestones in evolutionary computation highlight significant breakthroughs, including the formalization of genetic algorithms, evolution strategies, and other algorithms that transformed the field.

The next section outlines the types of evolutionary algorithms, beginning with Genetic Algorithms (GAs). These algorithms use selection, crossover, and mutation to evolve a population of solutions, with various variants and extensions improving their adaptability and efficiency. Genetic Programming (GP), a related approach, focuses on evolving programs instead of fixed-length solutions, offering flexibility in representation but posing challenges in terms of computational complexity and practical applications.

Evolution Strategies (ES) emphasize the role of mutation operators, with the most advanced technique being Covariance Matrix Adaptation

(CMA-ES), which dynamically adjusts mutation distribution based on past performance to optimize complex problems.

Differential Evolution (DE), another population-based algorithm, uses the differences between individuals to guide mutation, with its basic mechanisms focusing on simplicity and effectiveness. DE is widely applied and has several variants to address different optimization needs.

Part 1: (Very Short Questions)

1. What are the fundamental principles of early algorithms in evolutionary computation?

2. What were some key milestones in the evolution of evolutionary computation?

3. How do genetic algorithms function at a basic level?

4. What are some common variants and extensions of genetic algorithms?

5. How is genetic programming used to represent programs?

6. What are the main applications and challenges of genetic programming?

7. What role do mutation operators play in evolution strategies?

8. How does covariance matrix adaptation enhance evolution strategies?

9. What are the basic mechanisms of differential evolution?

10. Can you name a few variants and applications of differential evolution?

Part 2: (Short Questions)

1. What are the fundamental principles behind Genetic Algorithms (GAs)?

2. How does Genetic Programming differ from Genetic Algorithms in terms of program representation and application?

3. What is the role of mutation operators in Evolution Strategies, and how does Covariance Matrix Adaptation enhance their performance?

4. Can you describe the basic mechanisms of Differential Evolution and provide an example of its application?

5. What are some key milestones in the historical development of Evolutionary Computation?

Part 3: (Long Questions)

1. Discuss the historical development of evolutionary computation, including early algorithms and concepts that contributed to its foundation. Highlight key milestones in the evolution of this field and explain how these developments influenced modern evolutionary algorithms.

2. Explain the basic principles of Genetic Algorithms (GAs), including how they use natural selection processes to solve optimization problems. Describe the key components of GAs, such as selection, crossover, and mutation, and discuss various variants and extensions of GAs, including their impact on algorithm performance.

3. Explore the concept of Genetic Programming (GP) and its approach to evolving programs or expressions to solve complex problems. Discuss the methods for representing and encoding programs in GP, as well as the applications and challenges associated with GP, including issues like code bloat and evolving high-performance solutions.

4. Describe the principles of Evolution Strategies (ES) and their focus on optimization through mutation and recombination. Discuss the key mutation operators used in ES and how they influence the search process. Additionally, explain the concept of Covariance Matrix Adaptation (CMA) and its role in enhancing ES performance by adapting mutation distributions based on historical data.

5. Analyze the basic mechanisms of Differential Evolution (DE), including its core components such as mutation, crossover, and selection. Compare different variants of DE, such as DE/rand/1/bin and DE/best/1/bin, and discuss their specific applications in solving optimization problems, as well as any notable successes or challenges associated with these variants.

Part 4: (MCQs)

1. What is the fundamental principle of Genetic Algorithms (GAs)?

    a. Mimicking the behavior of neural networks

    b. Simulating the process of natural selection

    c. Utilizing gradient descent for optimization

    d. Implementing deterministic search techniques

2. Which of the following is NOT a common variant of Genetic Algorithms?

    a. Steady-State GA

    b. Island Model GA

    c. Evolutionary Strategy GA

    d. Multi-objective GA

3. In Genetic Programming, how are programs typically represented?

    a. As mathematical equations

    b. As tree structures

    c. As binary strings

    d. As linear sequences

4. Which of the following is a key challenge in Genetic Programming?

    a. Handling large datasets

    b. Maintaining diversity in the population

    c. Reducing computational cost

    d. Ensuring high precision in numerical solutions

5. What is a core feature of Evolution Strategies (ES)?

   a. Use of crossover operators

   b. Utilization of a fixed mutation rate

   c. Adaptation of the covariance matrix

   d. Binary encoding of solutions

6. Which mutation operator is commonly used in Evolution Strategies?

   a. Gaussian mutation

   b. Uniform mutation

   c. Polynomial mutation

   d. Bit-flip mutation

7. What is the primary mechanism used in Differential Evolution (DE) for generating new candidate solutions?

   a. Crossover and mutation

   b. Differential mutation

   c. Roulette wheel selection

   d. Tournament selection

8. Which of the following is NOT a variant of Differential Evolution?

   a. DE/rand/1/bin

   b. DE/best/1/exp

   c. DE/current-to-best/1/bin

   d. DE/multi/1/bin

9. What is a common application of Genetic Algorithms in optimization?

   a. Finding the shortest path in a graph

   b. Image recognition

   c. Language translation

   d. Time series forecasting

10. Which evolutionary computation method involves evolving a population of candidate solutions over time using selection, mutation, and crossover?

    a. Evolution Strategies

    b. Genetic Programming

    c. Differential Evolution

    d. Genetic Algorithms

Answer

1	2	3	4	5	6	7	8	9	10
b	c	b	b	c	a	b	d	a	d

CHAPTER 3

THEORETICAL UNDERPINNINGS

14. Introduction

Classes are bigger and more diverse in terms of students' abilities, motivations, and cultural backgrounds as a result of the recent growth, restructuring, and refinancing of the higher education industry. As a result of this shift, some professors are questioning their pedagogical assumptions and looking for ways to improve their students' ability to learn. The goal of this project was to overcome this obstacle by developing and perfecting several learning designs that other teachers could easily use and modify.

While many scholars acknowledge that teaching has always been an integral part of academia, they also note that this is not necessarily considered their primary responsibility showed that staying current with changes in one's field of study and making research contributions to those changes was many people's top goal. The development of one's teaching skills is ranked lower than other priorities in the university setting, according to his observation. This ranking is influenced by both institutional structures and reward systems, as well as individual choice. As a result, this setting might benefit greatly from a technology that enhances instruction and student achievement without necessitating that faculty members devote themselves entirely to the field of education.

Published in the Special Issue on LAMS and Learning Design, Volume 12, Issue 2, pages 51–61, 52 Teaching English with

Technology Academics have a greater need to make student learning a top priority in an era of increased student diversity. What this means is that teachers and administrators need to have some background knowledge on how and why students learn. Even the most accomplished educators, according to Gibbs' 2003 assessment, are frequently talented amateurs rather than rigorous professionals with any familiarity with the literature, and the majority of faculty members are less competent as educators than researchers. In higher education, there is still room for variation in terms of quality instruction since no coordinated tool has been developed to tackle this problem.

It is suggested that in order to deal with these challenges and keep standards current, new models of learning design should be investigated. There is a chance to combine the knowledge about how to promote effective learning with the need to reevaluate how we provide higher education in order to create learning designs that have more potential than some of the existing options. As a result, we came up with a plethora of specialised instructional plans for different fields.

This experiment demonstrated that academic staff may assist students in learning in novel ways by utilising scaffolded learning designs as pedagogical frameworks. Each lecturer can tailor the design to their students' needs by choosing or making the resources and supports that work best for them.

15. *Natural Selection and Evolutionary Theory*

The theory of evolution, one of the most significant intellectual revolutions in human history, completely transformed our perception of the cosmos and our place in it. Charles Darwin presented a unified theory of evolution and gathered substantial data to back it up. When Darwin lived, the majority of scientists had the firm belief that God created all living things and all of their adaptations. With the goal of documenting God's works, Linneaus laid the groundwork for modern taxonomy of living things. The similarities and contrasts among groups of species, which are generated by the branching process that generates the great tree of life (see Figure 1), were interpreted by philosophers and scientists in the early 19th century as indications of almighty design.

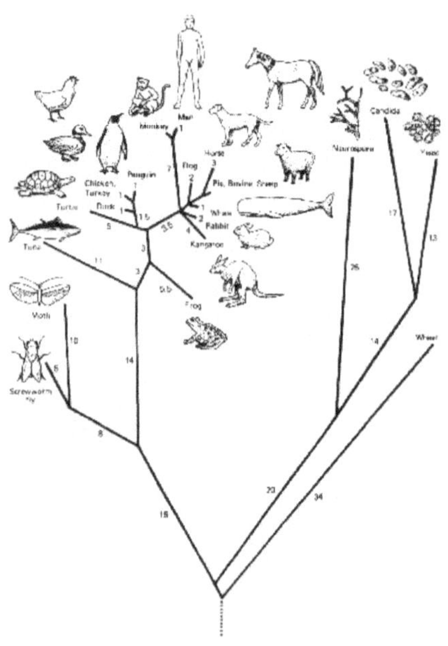

Source: - (Erten, 2023)

But by the 1800s, several natural historians were considering evolutionary change as a possible explanation for patterns seen in the natural world. The following were some of the prevalent philosophical views during Darwin's lifetime.

- Geologists were starting to make educated guesses that the earth was far older than what the Bible explains by creation, but no one knew for sure how ancient the earth was. As time went on, geologists gained a better understanding of strata, which are layers created by the gradual accumulation of sediments. The presence of younger layers on top of older strata indicated a temporal succession.

- By studying continuous, observable processes like erosion and the deposition of sediments, a school of thought known as uniformitarianism set out to unravel Earth's history, mainly as a result of the work of the great geologist Charles Lyell.

- The 18th and 19th centuries saw a steady stream of fossil discoveries. Naturalists initially mistook the fossils for those of some hitherto unexplained, potentially extinct species. However, it became clear as fossil discoveries persisted that no evidence of anything remotely like gigantic dinosaurs existed anywhere on Earth. The less similar fossils were to living species as one descended through the layers, as Cuvier noted as early as 1800.

- The idea that different groups of species would have evolved from one another was based on the idea that similarities between them indicated relatedness. Although they failed to offer a convincing explanation for the process of evolution, Darwin's intellectual forebears acknowledged the existence of evolutionary links between species.

Darwin's Theory

The following are the main points of Darwin's theory of evolution. Even before Darwin started his research on the "species problem," the first three concepts were being debated by naturalists both then and now. The theory of natural selection and a mountain of data supporting the idea of evolutionary change were Darwin's primary contributions. He elaborated on the ways in which evolution has changed our view of the origins of life and the variety of life in the modern world.

- Populations of related species undergo metamorphosis as a result of environmental and temporal factors. There is a noticeable change in the appearance or behaviour of populations in different parts of the world today, and current-day species representatives are distinct from their ancestors. The fossil record also shows these variations, lending credence to this theory.

- All living things have a common ancestor. Many species may arise from a single ancestor population as a result of natural selection. If we go back far enough in time, we can find shared ancestry between any two species. We share a common ancestor with chimpanzees and whales about eight million years ago, kangaroos and humans more than 100 million years ago, and chimpanzees and chimps and whales about 60 million years ago. The common ancestry of all classified organisms explains their shared traits: Genetic inheritance from a common ancestor is the cause of their shared traits.

- Darwin believed that evolution is a slow and steady process. The fact that no naturalist during Darwin's time had noticed the abrupt emergence of a new species and the lengthy periods of slow change in creatures in the fossil record provided evidence supporting this hypothesis.

The Process of Natural Selection

Darwin's process of natural selection has four components.

Variation: Individuals within populations of organisms display behavioural and morphological diversity. Size, hair colour, physical features, vocal qualities, and progeny number are all areas where these variances can manifest. The number of eyeballs in vertebrates is one example of a characteristic that does not vary much from one person to the next.

Inheritance: There are certain characteristics that are reliably passed down from parents to children. Such features are inherited, in contrast to those whose heritability is limited and which are heavily impacted by external factors.

1. Rapid increase in the population. Annual population growth often outstrips available resources, causing resource scarcity in most areas. There is a significant amount of death in every generation.

2. Two, distinct ways of surviving and passing on genes. Success in the fight for limited resources is directly proportional to the number of children produced by individuals with the right set of characteristics.

3. The conflict for resources, which Darwin referred to as the "struggle for existence," changes the frequency of features

within the population from one generation to the next by favouring individuals with some variants over others. So, this is how natural selection works. "Adaptations" are the characteristics that help certain species outperform others in terms of reproduction.

4. A characteristic can only be subject to natural selection if it is both heritably variable and advantageous in resource competition. In order for a trait to undergo natural selection, at least one of these conditions must be satisfied. (Other evolutionary mechanisms have been found since Darwin's time that may cause such features to alter).

15.1. Concepts of Fitness and Survival

"Fitness" and "survival" are key concepts in evolutionary biology and are often intertwined when explaining how species adapt and evolve over time.

1. Fitness

In an evolutionary context, fitness refers to the ability of an organism to survive, reproduce, and pass on its genes to the next generation. Fitness is often measured by the number of offspring an organism produces that survive to reproduce themselves.

Relative Fitness: This measures an individual's reproductive success in comparison to others in the population. It's not just about survival, but about how well an organism's traits enable it to reproduce in its specific environment.

Factors Affecting Fitness: Fitness depends on various traits such as:

- Physical strength and health.

- Ability to find food, mates, and shelter.

- Resistance to disease or environmental challenges.

2. Survival

Survival refers to an organism's ability to stay alive long enough to reproduce. However, survival itself is not the only measure of evolutionary success; an organism must also reproduce to contribute to the next generation.

Survival of the Fittest: This term, coined by Herbert Spencer after reading Darwin's work, captures the idea that those best adapted to their environment tend to survive and reproduce. However, "fittest" doesn't necessarily mean the strongest or fastest. It means those best suited to their environment in terms of surviving and passing on genes.

The Relationship Between Fitness and Survival

- **Survival alone is insufficient**: An organism that survives but does not reproduce will not pass on its genes, meaning its "fitness" is effectively zero.

- **Reproduction is key:** Traits that enhance reproduction—whether through better mating strategies, better survival of offspring, or other means—directly increase an organism's fitness.

- **Natural Selection:** Over generations, individuals with traits that increase fitness tend to become more common in the population, because they are more likely to survive and reproduce. This is the basis of natural selection, the mechanism of evolution described by Darwin.

15.2. Genetic Drift and Gene Flow

Gene flow and genetic drift are two processes among three different necessary processes required for the evolution of species. Both terms are different, however, they are interconnected too. Gene flow focuses on migrating the genes from one gene pool to another pool, while genetic drift depends on the allelic frequencies, an alternative form of genes.

Definition of gene flow and genetic drift

- Gene flow can be defined as the transmission of genes or genetic material from gene pool on species to another gene pool by interbreeding and resulting in alteration of the recipient gene pool. Gene flow is also known as gene migration

- Genetic drift can be described as a strong effect of instability considering the allelic frequencies of small populations. It is generally caused due to random events, errors in allele selection, or sampling. Genetic drift occurs mainly in tiny populations because, in more significant populations, allelic frequencies mostly remain stable, freeing environmental factors like natural selection

Possible causes of gene flow and genetic drift

Gene flow and genetic drift are connected, but they differ in occurrence, size, variations, evolution, etc. The possible reasons of gene flow and sense on several aspects are mentioned below:

- **Reason of occurrence:** Gene flow occurs through continuous interbreeding or cross-breeding between two nearby populations whereas genetic drift occurs by the sudden constant sampling errors, elimination, or imbalance in the allelic frequencies of a small group of genes.

- **Size of population:** The acquisition of a process that genes undertake is highly dependent on the population of a species or group. The gene groups with smaller finite people tend to possess genetic drift. In contrast, the infinite populations or bigger groups perform gene flow, altering the recipient group's gene pool.

- **Evolution:** The evolution of new genotypes and traits occurs through gene flow and drift, and the only difference is how growth happens. In gene flow, a shift occurs with the immigration of genes to another species, composing their gene pool and causing variants in evolution. In genetic drift, the composition in adjacent populations is done through several effects: the bottleneck and the founder.

- **Genetic variations:** The variations occur in gene flow primarily due to the size of their group. Many genetic transfers are seen due to gene flow because it occurs due to pure environmental immigration of molecules of gametes, which interbred with new populations, and the development of variations of allelic occur. This is the process through which alleles are formed. While in genetic drift, due to its sudden and short-term occurrence and small size, the evolution of variations might not take place.

16. Fitness Landscapes

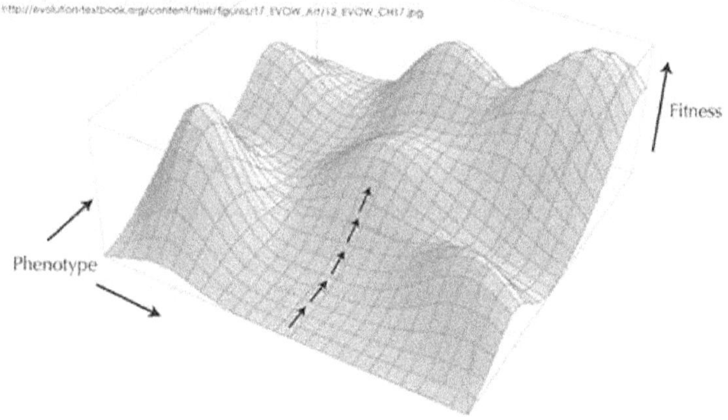

Source: - (Brand, 2023)

Seeing a fitness landscape animation for the first time was in Man and Nature (1969) by Garrett Hardin. Its message of avoiding becoming overly specialised and adapted at one local peak of fitness became crystal clear to me as I realised that distant mountain ranges of opportunity were there, but that I would have to move "downhill" into less fit regions to attain them. I lost trust in perfection.

Fitness landscapes, often called "adaptive landscapes," keep cropping up when people are attempting to explain the function of evolution or innovation in complex environments. Marvin Minsky and Seymour Papert's seminal critique of early AI optimism states that seemingly intelligent entities will "hill climb" to local heights of illusory optimality and become stuck there. A celebration of the "adjacent possible" and its role in creativity, Where Good beliefs Come From had its origins in fitness landscapes, which complexity theorist Stuart Kauffman employed from 1993 to 2000 to illustrate his beliefs on the "adjacent possible."

Sewell Wright, a pioneer in the field of population genetics, was the brains behind fitness landscapes (1889-1988). By visualising what might push an evolutionary "path" downward from a local high towards alternative possibilities, he was able to illustrate and explain how biological populations avoid becoming trapped by a peak in 1932. Take a look at these six of his diagrams.

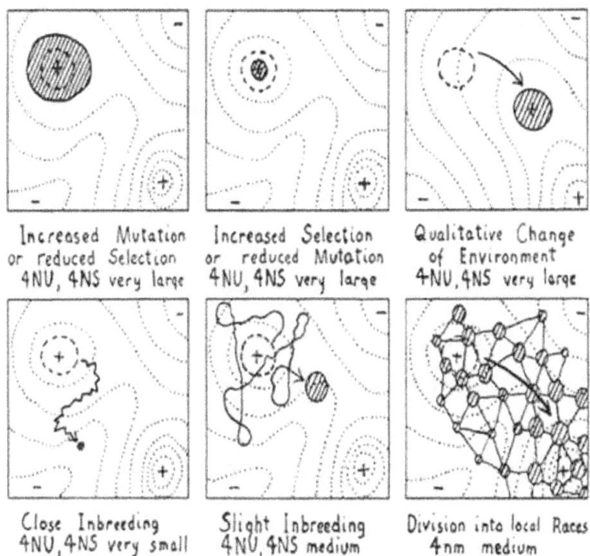

Source: - (Brand, 2023)

In the first two, we see how small populations with a high mutation rate and weak selection pressure can force a species to stay close to its local fitness maximum, while in the third, we see how large populations with weak selection and high mutation rates can force a species to expand its range. The third diagram shows how a population adapts to a changing environment.

Ineffective wandering is an example of a tiny population's response to inbreeding, as seen in the bottom row. Wright considered the last diagram, which shows how a species might split into many interdependent races, to be the most effective means of discovery. That tumultuous mob is good at exploring and reacting to opportunities.

There is a great deal of economic expression in fitness landscapes. To illustrate how, say, a tropical jungle on land and an isolated island in the ocean have developed differently, there is no greater illustration. Dense and "rugged" with sharp peaks and valleys, the jungle isolates many species on the tip of their very specific peaks. The island's little flora and fauna are like a landscape of undulating hills, where different species meander aimlessly, eventually giving rise to, example, a wide variety of finches described by Darwin. In the face of mainland invaders, the island's flora and fauna "lazily" become helpless.

16.1. Multi-modal Fitness Landscapes

This function generates multi-modal fitness landscapes based on distance measures. The fitness is the minimal distance to several reference individuals or centers. Hence, each reference individual is an optimum of the landscape.

An optimisation problem's difficulty rises due, in large part, to the fitness landscape's multimodality. It is evident that a high dimensionality makes the search more difficult due to the presence of several local optima. On its own, this feature doesn't tell us much; to get useful results, we need to include it with other variables, such as the distances between local optima and the global optimum or the diameters of their attraction basins. Using two very effective EAs, Differential Evolution and Covariance Matrix Adaptation, we present a real-valued fitness landscape analysis approach that delivers such comprehensive data and explore its consequences.

A technique for analysing fitness landscapes across many modalities using the notion of attraction basins for binary-valued functions. In order to determine the complexity of a landscape for a given operator, they propose an algorithm that, given a landscape and a local search operator chosen for the specific characteristics of the EA being studied, calculates the size of the attraction basins and the number of local optima. In order to compare various EAs based on their local optima distribution estimates, we built a more general analysis algorithm for real-valued issues using the foundational principles of this work. This method makes use of a generic local search operator.

In multi-modal fitness landscapes, the function of exploration vs exploitation is another essential notion. While exploitation is concerned with improving solutions in areas that have already demonstrated potential, exploration is concerned with exploring new parts of the fitness landscape. The key to thriving in a multi-modal environment is finding a happy medium between the two. An algorithm can become caught in a local optimum if it is overly exploited, and it will be inefficient while trying to discover a high-quality solution if it is overly explored.

Key Characteristics of Multi-modal Fitness Landscapes:

- **Local and Global Optima**: A multi-modal landscape consists of several local optima, which represent good but not necessarily the best solutions. The global optimum, representing the highest or lowest point depending on the problem type, may be far from these local optima. This structure makes it hard for optimization algorithms to distinguish between local and global peaks.

- **Deceptive Regions**: Some portions of the landscape may look promising at first (steep ascents or descents), but ultimately result in bad solutions. These misleading zones can readily trap optimisation algorithms, forcing them to converge prematurely to local optima rather than continue to search for better solutions.

- **High Dimensionality**: Many real-world situations involving multi-modal landscapes take place in three-dimensional environments. This enhances the complexity of the terrain, frequently leading to many additional optima and complicating the search process.

Applications of Multi-modal Fitness Landscapes:

Multi-modal landscapes are not just a theoretical concept—they appear in many practical optimization problems across various domains:

- **Neural Network Training**: Neural network training frequently involves complex multi-modal loss landscapes with several local minima. Proper optimisation is critical to prevent local minima, which may create subpar models.

- **Engineering Design**: Multi-modal fitness landscapes are frequently used to solve complex engineering optimisation challenges such as aerodynamic design or circuit design. Different designs may perform well in certain settings, but only one is globally ideal.

- **Protein Folding**: In computational biology, the protein folding issue is distinguished by a highly multi-modal fitness landscape, where various configurations of a protein are feasible, but only one corresponds to the best stable and functional structure.

16.2. Fitness Landscape Analysis Techniques

The 2013 survey that appeared in the Information Sciences journal served as a springboard for this one. There wasn't a tonne of action in the evolutionary computation community regarding fitness landscape analysis back then. Despite a lot of theory and research on fitness landscape analysis, the article claims that "very few techniques are used in practice... " The goal of this study is to improve decision-making about the adoption of suitable metaheuristics by reviving interest in the area of understanding difficult optimisation problems. It is evident that fitness landscape analysis is once again a hot topic, since the number of papers covering the topic is increasing and every major evolutionary computation conference has tutorials, seminars, and special sessions dedicated to the subject.

- **Beyond Fitness Landscapes:** Sewell Wright first proposed the idea of a fitness landscape in 1932 during a genetics symposium. He proposed a two-dimensional fitness contour map as a means of better visualising the complex evolutionary processes. The broad use of fitness landscapes outside of biological and computational evolution has led many researchers to opt for more generic terms such as search space analysis, exploratory landscape analysis, or simply landscape analysis.

- **Violation Landscapes:** Presented a new perspective on fitness landscapes for limited search spaces—a violation landscape. A violation landscape is constructed using the same components as a fitness landscape; however, instead of a fitness function, which assesses the extent to which a solution violates the issue constraints, a violation function is utilised. An additional landscape perspective, the violation landscape, is defined above the choice variable space to augment the fitness landscape. By comparing violation landscapes to fitness landscapes, we can gain a better understanding of limited optimisation issues and their characteristics. Measurements for describing violation landscapes in connection to fitness landscapes are described in Technique.

- **Dynamic and Coupled Fitness Landscapes:** Despite the fact that landscapes are constantly changing, most analyses of them still operate under the assumption that the environment is static. Two situations where landscape dynamics have been investigated are coevolution, in which landscapes are connected and impact one another, and applications where the objective function evolves over time (as a result of changes in the issue environment).

- **Error Landscapes:** Optimisation tasks are an aspect of training neural networks (NNs), and one of them is finding the weight values that minimise the network model's error during training. You can learn more about the characteristics of a particular NN weight optimisation problem by looking at the loss or error landscape, which is comparable to a fitness landscape. When compared to other black-box optimisation problems, NN weight optimisation has a few important differences that impact landscape analysis.

Advances in Landscape Analysis

Recent method proposals, studies on sampling, and the reliability of landscape analysis are all included in this part, which aims to contribute to the field. Prior surveys should be perused by the reader to familiarise themselves with the ideas and jargon of fitness landscape analysis.

Techniques for Landscape Analysis

The initial survey's goal was to provide researchers with easier access to the methods by providing clear descriptions of each method and drawing attention to characteristics that impact their practical application.

- **Technique:** the name of the technique, citation and extensions (where the technique was adapted in subsequent studies).

- **Year:** the year the technique was first introduced in published form.

- **Focus:** refers to what is measured or predicted by the technique.

- **Assumptions:** any significant assumptions on which the technique is based.

- **Description:** summary of how the technique works.

- **Result:** describes the form of output produced by the technique (numerical, graphical, etc.).

Sampling and Robustness of Measures

The majority of methods for analysing landscapes rely on sampling the search space. Both the sample size and the sampling procedure influence the results of the analysis when thinking about the impact of sampling.

Applications of Landscape Analysis

In recent years, landscape analysis has become more popular as a tool for automated algorithm configuration and selection, performance prediction, and comprehending complicated problems and algorithm behaviour.

Understanding and Explaining Algorithm Behaviour

Competitive experimental findings on a narrow selection of benchmark tasks are typically the basis for the introduction of new metaheuristic algorithms. The investigations don't provide any scientific explanation for the algorithm's success or failure on the given problems, which is a major drawback of this approach.

Algorithm Performance Prediction

It is possible to deduce the algorithmic components of most metaheuristics, but the resulting behaviour is frequently surprising. In order to forecast how well an algorithm will work, landscape analysis can be employed to identify broad problem characteristics. When it comes to the larger goal of automated algorithm selection, these models play a significant role. Here are a few examples of how machine learning has been applied improve forecast algorithm performance using landscape features:

From its theoretical roots in evolutionary computation, landscape analysis has emerged as a popular method for optimisation and, more lately, machine learning. This overview of current trends in the subject details many new approaches to landscape analysis as well as works in the areas of sampling and measure robustness. The survey also highlights approaches to automate algorithm design and selection, characterise algorithm behaviour, forecast algorithm performance, and understand complex situations using landscape analysis. Thanks to optimisation and machine learning, we can put our faith in technology to solve real-world problems; landscape analysis is an essential tool for making algorithms more predictable.

17. Convergence and Diversity

College life may be a maze. Not even individuals with extensive experience in the field can adequately describe its inner workings, including how it is financed, how its institutions are run, and how students are expected to make the most of the opportunities presented by a university education.1 While estimates put the number of bachelor's degrees awarded by UK institutions at over 50,000 and the number of master's degrees at over 20,000, the exact number of degree programs offered by the 45 European countries that have joined the Bologna process is unknown. The majority of those countries' higher education systems cannot be accurately described by more than a handful of individuals. The sphere of higher learning, however, is as significant. In many nations, nearly half of all youths will soon have the opportunity to attend college, thanks to the dramatic increase in student enrolment in recent years. They will be attending some of the most economically powerful schools in their hometowns, and those businesses are well aware that the majority of their employees will require the education and training that these students provide. The vast majority of these graduates will not stop their education after earning a bachelor's degree; rather, they will continue their education at their alma mater or another institution to ensure that they are competent in their chosen fields, whether that's through a master's degree, a doctorate, or even just a few refresher courses. The commercial and industrial sectors will become more dependent on university-based research and innovation as a result of alternative information transfer mechanisms.

As a last point, colleges and universities are vital to a democratic and civil society. Higher education should be a priority for the government for all these reasons. From time to time, political analysts and academics will argue that universities should not be run by the government. The reality is that the vast majority of universities in the US, including the so-called private institutions, depend on public funding for research and student services; there are very few universities that can be considered truly "private" in this context. Their "output" of competent and well-informed citizens is essential to the well-being of any civilisation, hence the state would continue to support them regardless of the number. Therefore, colleges and universities need to figure out how to live, preferably through collaboration instead of competition.

The Bologna process is an evolving symbol of the repercussions of these new partnerships between governments, civil society, and universities. One fundamental shift, sometimes characterised by the depressing phrase "massification," from an elite-only university system to a system for the masses has resulted in new kinds of interactions. In the past, when there was less mobility of students between institutions (during courses or for second degrees), colleges could depend on a shared body of knowledge. This was especially true when university systems were smaller and served mostly the upper and middle classes. No matter how strange or complicated a certain school's procedures and policies were, it didn't matter because everyone who had attended that school could comprehend them and everyone else trusted that they were excellent. Academic achievement in the universities of Athens, Bologna, Cracow, Heidelberg, Oxford, or Paris was apparent.

Diversity No one really cares which part of the world is the most diverse, but everyone can agree that the languages, countries, and regions of Europe have a long and storied history that they are justifiably proud of. Legendary or otherwise, heroes from politics, literature, or conflict are commonplace in every nation. Classical Greek had an impact on imperial Rome, and so on throughout history; what is remarkable about any list of the great men and women of European nations is the degree to which they have all been shaped—both directly and indirectly—by their exposure to the art, literature, history, and language of other European nations. Classical Renaissance, Enlightenment rationalism, and the Romantic movement were all born in Europe, but they took shape and gained traction through translation and reinterpretation in many languages and cultures, as well as in the context of diverse national histories.

Thus, Europe has a historical tradition of preserving cultural variety while nevertheless adhering to a common conceptual framework. In the past, variety has been an asset, paving the way for and even stimulating innovations in policy, technology, and the pursuit of the human spirit. True, it has also served as a catalyst for divisiveness, heated discussion, and even bloodshed on other times. The religious wars of the seventeenth century, the persecution of Catholics in Protestant England, the Inquisition, the mediaeval Provence persecution of the Cathars, the antisemitism that has plagued Europe from the Middle Ages to the Holocaust, and the conflicts in the Balkans in the 1990s are just a few examples. All of these instances highlight the inherent danger of diversity in the context of intolerance, but they also show how understanding and tolerance of diversity can produce some of the most magnificent literary and musical creations.

Diversity in the academic sector tends to have less dramatic effects, yet scathing arguments do arise. Higher education in Europe, however, has taken numerous distinct paths to its current state, with a system that encompasses a wide variety of institutions. Oxford and Cambridge are examples of collegiate universities that emerged in mediaeval Europe and continue to this day. Collegiate universities combined on-campus housing for faculty and students with classroom instruction and library research. This concept worked successfully with a limited curriculum and served primarily the needs of the clergy and a select group of other academic vocations. This version lasted all the way into the late 18th and early 19th century.

Despite all the focus on the Bologna process since 1999, it is evident that it does not cover all the difficulties and developments impacting European higher education right now. In fact, Bologna is only indirectly or even indirectly related to many of the changes that are vaguely attributed to it, usually by angry university professors. Bologna has had a negligible impact on the variety of European higher education institutions and the systems they are a part of. The decline in early-level funding for most nations' rising student populations, the shift from an elite to a mass system, and the subsequent increase in student enrolment have all been far more consequential. Bologna may have been less of a driver of these shifts and more of a reaction to them.

Concurrently, Bologna was motivated by some admirable goals, such as making European higher education more accessible and appealing to the general public, increasing student mobility within and between European nations, and preparing students from Europe to be successful citizens and workers in the modern world. Those are praiseworthy goals, at least to everyone who isn't a staunch Euro-skeptic. Historiographers will remember that universities first emerged in mediaeval Europe, at the time of the "wandering scholars"—among them, Erasmus, the namesake of the EU's student mobility program, stands tall.

17.1. Diversity Maintenance Strategies

Increased output and teamwork are two benefits of a diversified workforce. Enhancing the office atmosphere and fostering workplace creativity can be achieved through the blending of many cultures, experiences, and ideas. One drawback of a diverse workforce is the increased potential for religious tensions and misunderstandings stemming from different worldviews.

Also, management needs to be creative if they want to handle diversity in the workplace well. With the right leadership in place, a diverse workplace can produce synergy like never before. "Diversity" is a catch-all word for many complex issues.

Workers from different racial and ethnic backgrounds, as well as those with different socioeconomic statuses, religious beliefs, and so on, make up a varied workforce. Diversity may also help your staff adapt to a more complicated external environment, which can only improve your business. Nevertheless, it could also prolong certain problems.

Understanding Corporate Diversity in the Workplace

Creating a plan to increase diversity inside the organisation is the initial stage. When companies actively seek for and recruit candidates with a wide range of backgrounds, experiences, and skill sets, they are fostering an organisational culture that values diversity. To what end does diversity in the workplace serve? Using the knowledge and perspectives of as many people as possible to advance innovation, prosperity, and advancement.

Furthermore, because identification is an essential part of organisational diversity, it is imperative that contemporary businesses recruit, retain, and advance individuals whose backgrounds and experiences mirror those of the communities and markets they serve. In today's business world, how can diversity goals like representation be met? There must be a plan, a change in mindset, a determination, and responsibility on the part of the company.

<u>**Role of Workplace Diversity Management**</u>

What steps have you taken to ensure that your workplace is diverse? Equal opportunity and diversity in the workplace are goals that, in a sense, will remain constants for as long as your company does. Diversity programs will be around for a long time, and CEOs and other corporate leaders should make them a priority for the foreseeable future.

Attaining complete leadership support, which should be supported by data and statistics, should be the first step for interested managers and leaders. If you want to find out where your firm stands in terms of diversity and equality, you can hire outside experts or apply your own survey methods. The findings might surprise key stakeholders.

Workplace Diversity Strategies: How to put Diversity, Inclusion, and Equity into Action

Locate data for programs promoting equality and diversity Think about the data needs of your inclusion and diversity programs first. Is it essential for your company to have dedicated diversity and inclusion professionals, as is common these days, or will HR handle this?

How much money will you need to manage diversity initiatives? Should money be set aside to establish employee resource networks or to make a website to back them up?

Could you use the services of a consultant? To figure out the best approach to building the tools needed to assist your diversity management initiatives, meet with important stakeholders throughout the organisation.

- **Set multicultural goals and responsibility for change and remain proactive**

  Which part of the "how to handle diversity" question's second portion should we address? Make an effort to be methodical in your pursuits. Using lofty but still attainable standards, establish and hold your organisation accountable for attainable diversity goals.

  Above all else, do not bury these objectives in secret corporate paperwork. If you want your company to take pride in its diversity, inclusion, and equality efforts, it's a good idea to let everyone in the office know about them. This will keep everyone informed about your current activities.

- **Seek out various mindsets by hiring diverse people**

  One of the best times to implement diversity strategies is during the hiring process, when potential employees are still in the hiring phase. Having well-defined expectations, guidelines, and targets for your recruiters and HR professionals will help you bring in a varied pool of talent that will enhance your company's performance.

  Also, keep in mind that this should be applicable to positions beyond entry-level ones. Make sure that your diversity and inclusion initiatives reach all levels of staff, from entry-level workers to upper management (and beyond).

- **Set up diversity, inclusion, and equity training**

  Knowledge gained through inclusive education is crucial to effective diversity management. Achieving genuine diversity in the workplace takes time. Access to diversity and continuing education programs should be available to all employees. Beyond that, check if these activities still contribute to their annual objectives.

- **Create a leadership team with a wide range of expertise**

  The kind of vision that a contemporary business needs can be provided by a diverse management team. When a company's leadership, board of directors, and senior management don't reflect the diversity of the community they serve, it will be difficult to attract and retain customers. This is why equality and diversity must start at the top of any organisation.

  Additionally, aim to start at the top of your organisation when contemplating diversity in company management.

- **Decide on initiatives**

  A key part of figuring out how to handle diversity at work is figuring out what organisations will do. Once again, this process will involve everyone from the CEO on down.

  Get the upper management and the workforce together for a meeting to discuss the current state of affairs and figure out where to start making real management changes. When it comes to diversity management, there is no "one-size-fits-all" solution because every company is different, particularly multinational corporations. Although it will be beneficial in the end, it will require considerable thought, preparation, and execution.

- **Emphasize inclusion structure and procedures**

  The final stage of leading a multicultural team? Maintain a policy of equality, inclusiveness, and diversity as a top organisational objective. Just to fulfil administrative and compliance obligations or to tick a few boxes on their company's mission, far too many organisations launch diversity and inclusion projects.

  Make sure your engagement policies and systems don't end up as dusty old relics in the employee handbook. Make sure they are current and adapt them according to what is required by the situation and the environment. Everyone who matters to your success—your employees, your customers, and the world at large—requires it. That is why you should prioritise equality, diversity, and inclusion.

- **Policy evaluation**

  While it is the goal of most companies' basic principles to treat all employees fairly, this does not necessarily lead to more diversity in the workplace. If businesses want to hire a more diverse workforce, they need to rethink their vacation, time off, and feedback policies.

  While most companies respect regular holidays, those that truly embrace diversity in the workplace will also acknowledge the many religious festivals observed by their employees and offer more flexible leave policies to accommodate them.

The Bottom Line

Put simply, the need for diversity in the workplace is increasing as the global economy becomes more interconnected. Having a diversified workforce can be crucial for companies looking to stay competitive in the long run.

17.2. Convergence Analysis and Metrics

In machine learning, a convergence analysis is used to find out how close an algorithm gets to its ideal solution, usually by tracking the loss function or the accuracy as time goes on. To stabilise the model's performance as it learns from the data, convergence aims to strike a balance between the speed and reliability of obtaining the ideal parameters or the minimum of the objective function. The optimisation technique, learning rate, data properties, and model complexity are some of the elements that impact convergence.

Metrics like accuracy, precision, recall, F1-score, and AUC (Area Under the Curve) track an algorithm's convergence in supervised learning. When training a model, it is possible to evaluate its fit to the training data using metrics like loss, which can be either mean squared error for regression or categorical cross-entropy for classification. The loss function should rapidly decrease as the model learns and converges; if it stagnates or oscillates, it might mean that convergence is sluggish or that the model is not tuned properly.

Convergence analysis is particularly important in optimisation approaches such as gradient descent, which aims to find the minimum of a loss function. The learning rate is an important feature of convergence since it affects how quickly or slowly an algorithm reaches its minimum. A high learning rate may lead the model to exceed its minimum, whereas a low learning rate may result in sluggish convergence. Learning rate scheduling, momentum, and adaptive algorithms such as Adam or RMSprop are utilised to accelerate convergence.

Metrics for Monitoring Convergence

- **Training Loss and Validation Loss**: The loss function is one of the most popular convergence measures, and it is tracked throughout both the training and validation stages. As the model learns, the training loss usually reduces. The validation loss aids in determining generalisability. If the validation loss begins to diverge or grow while the training loss continues to drop, this might suggest overfitting, which occurs when the model performs well on training data but badly on unknown data.

- **Accuracy, Precision, Recall, and F1 Score**: Common metrics for classification tasks include accuracy, recall, precision, and the F1 score. When it comes to unbalanced datasets, accuracy is a good indicator of how well the model performed overall, while precision and recall show how well it performed on individual classes. F1 scores integrate recall and accuracy into one measure. You can see how well the model is converging on the training and validation sets by looking at these indicators.

- **Learning Curves**: Plotting the learning curves, which reflect the loss or accuracy across the number of epochs, gives a visual aid for analysing convergence. A typical curve will indicate a significant decline in loss during the early epochs, followed by a plateau when convergence occurs. If the training and validation curves diverge, it might indicate overfitting or underfitting, necessitating hyperparameter modifications such as regularisation or early termination.

- **Early Stopping**: Early stopping is a convergence approach in which training is ended once the validation loss has stopped improving after a predetermined number of epochs. This helps to prevent overfitting and guarantees that the model converges at the point when its generalisation performance is maximised.

<u>Convergence in Deep Learning:</u>

Convergence in deep learning models gets increasingly difficult owing to the high number of parameters and the loss functions' non-convex character. The disappearing and ballooning gradient difficulties that arise in deep neural networks might impede convergence. These problems occur when gradients are too tiny (vanish) or too huge (explode), preventing the model from learning successfully. Gradient clipping, careful initialisation, and the use of designs such as residual networks (ResNets) can all assist to alleviate these issues and increase convergence.

Another aspect of deep learning is the use of dropout and batch normalisation. Dropout prevents overfitting and guarantees that the model learns resilient representations by randomly deactivating certain neurones during training. Batch normalisation, on the other hand, normalises the inputs to each layer, accelerating and stabilising convergence by decreasing internal covariate movements.

18. Chapter Summary

This chapter delves into key concepts of natural selection and evolutionary theory, laying the groundwork for understanding evolutionary algorithms. Central to the theory are the concepts of fitness and survival, where organisms best adapted to their environment thrive and pass on their genes. In evolutionary algorithms, this translates to the most optimal solutions surviving through iterations. Genetic drift (random changes in gene frequencies) and gene flow (transfer of genetic information between populations) are also important, as they impact population diversity and adaptation over time.

The discussion then moves to fitness landscapes, which represent the solution space where fitness values (or objective function values) are evaluated. Multi-modal fitness landscapes contain multiple peaks and valleys, corresponding to local and global optima, making optimization more challenging. The chapter also introduces fitness landscape analysis techniques, used to understand the topography of these landscapes and guide algorithmic decisions.

The chapter addresses the critical balance between convergence and diversity in evolutionary algorithms. Convergence refers to the population of solutions becoming more similar over time, ideally toward an optimal solution. However, premature convergence can trap the algorithm in local optima. To prevent this, diversity maintenance strategies are essential, ensuring a broad exploration of the search space. Techniques like niching, crowding, and fitness sharing help maintain population variety.

Finally, convergence analysis and metrics are discussed, offering tools to measure how well and quickly an evolutionary algorithm converges toward the optimal solution, while considering the trade-off between exploration and exploitation in the search process.

Part 1: (Very Short Questions)

1. What is the concept of fitness in evolutionary theory?

2. How does genetic drift affect allele frequencies in a population?

3. What role does gene flow play in evolutionary change?

4. What defines a multi-modal fitness landscape?

5. How can fitness landscape analysis techniques be applied in evolutionary studies?

6. What are some common diversity maintenance strategies in evolutionary algorithms?

7. How is convergence measured in evolutionary computations?

8. What is the significance of fitness landscapes in evolutionary theory?

9. How does fitness landscape analysis contribute to understanding evolutionary processes?

10. What metrics are used for analyzing convergence in evolutionary algorithms?

Part 2: (Short Questions)

1. What is the role of fitness and survival in the process of natural selection?

2. How do genetic drift and gene flow influence evolutionary outcomes?

3. What distinguishes multi-modal fitness landscapes from other types of fitness landscapes?

4. What are some common techniques used to analyze fitness landscapes?

5. What are diversity maintenance strategies, and why are they important in evolutionary algorithms?

Part 3: (Long Questions)

1. How do the concepts of fitness and survival contribute to the process of natural selection, and how does evolutionary theory explain the adaptive changes in populations over time?

2. Expzain the roles of genetic drift and gene flow in shaping genetic diversity within populations, and discuss their implications for the evolutionary trajectory of a species.

3. What are fitness landscapes, and how do multi-modal fitness landscapes and fitness landscape analysis techniques contribute to our understanding of evolutionary processes?

4. Describe the significance of convergence and diversity in evolutionary biology, including strategies for maintaining diversity and methods for analyzing convergence.

5. Outline the techniques used in fitness landscape analysis and discuss their applications, advantages, and limitations in understanding evolutionary dynamics.

Part 4: (MCQs)

1. What does "fitness" refer to in evolutionary biology?

   a. The physical strength of an organism

   b. An organism's ability to survive and reproduce

   c. The speed at which an organism evolves

   d. The mutation rate of a population

2. Which of the following best describes genetic drift?

   a. A process where beneficial traits become more common due to survival advantages

   b. Random fluctuations in allele frequencies in a population

   c. The introduction of new genes into a population from another population

   d. A force that increases genetic diversity in a large population

3. Gene flow can be described as:

   a. The process where certain genes are eliminated from the gene pool

   b. The transfer of genetic material between populations

   c. The isolation of populations due to geographic barriers

   d. The development of new species within a population

4. In fitness landscapes, what is meant by "multi-modal" landscapes?

   a. Landscapes with a single peak representing the highest fitness

   b. Landscapes with multiple peaks representing different local fitness optima

c. Landscapes that fluctuate rapidly over time

d. Landscapes with low diversity and convergence towards a single solution

5. Which of the following is a technique for analyzing fitness landscapes?

a. Convergence analysis

b. Genetic drift measurement

c. Ruggedness and smoothness analysis

d. Survival of the fittest

6. What is the primary challenge in multi-modal fitness landscapes for evolutionary algorithms?

a. Finding the global optimum

b. Maintaining population diversity

c. Avoiding genetic drift

d. Ensuring gene flow between populations

7. Diversity maintenance strategies in evolutionary algorithms are important because:

a. They speed up convergence

b. They prevent premature convergence to suboptimal solutions

c. They eliminate genetic drift

d. They remove low-fitness individuals from the population

8. Which of the following is an example of a diversity maintenance strategy?

a. Mutation suppression

b. Elitism

c. Crowding or niching

d. Gene flow prevention

9. Convergence analysis is typically used to measure:

    a. The diversity of a population over time

    b. How quickly an evolutionary algorithm finds an optimal solution

    c. The rate of gene flow between populations

    d. The mutation rate in a population

10. A high level of convergence in an evolutionary algorithm typically suggests:

    a. High diversity in the population

    b. Premature convergence to a suboptimal solution

    c. Effective mutation strategies

    d. Continuous exploration of new solutions

Answer

1	2	3	4	5	6	7	8	9	10
b	b	b	b	c	a	b	c	b	b

CHAPTER 4

DESIGNING EVOLUTIONARY COMPUTATION SYSTEMS

19. Introduction

Evolutionary Computation has been widely used for design generation in the last ten or so years. Artists have used evolution to generate aesthetically pleasing shapes, architects have evolved new building plans from the ground up, and designers have improved specific parts of their designs using evolution. Computer scientists have constructed the morphologies and control systems of artificial life.

While there is some collaboration between disciplines, it appears that many researchers work in the dark about the closely related work done by others, and this is despite the fact that researchers in these various application areas often work in isolation from one another. To address this, this paper will try to unify the many facets of this field of study under one umbrella: Origins of Form.

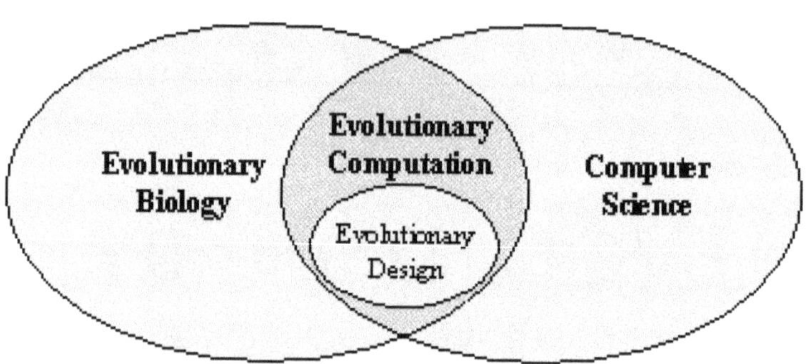

Source: - (Bentley, 2024)

Research spanning multiple disciplines is nothing new to Evolutionary Computation. The field as a whole owes its existence to the pioneers who attempted to bridge the gap between computer science and evolutionary biology (for example, see figure 1), such as Holland, Rechenberg, and Fogel.

Unfortunately, it seems that many academics have a propensity to become intellectually territorialist when they get overly focused on a single field of study and want to separate themselves by highlighting ever-widening gaps. This essay aspires to convince some of these barriers to be eliminated by highlighting the shared but often viewed as separate parts of research.

Therefore, this paper suggests that the field of study known as "Evolutionary Design" should cover four separate areas: Artificial Life Forms, Creative Evolutionary Design, Evolutionary Art, and Evolutionary Design Optimisation.

Some academics' work does not fit cleanly into a single category, but rather into two or even three, as is common with any form of classification scheme. Such work is also examined in this publication. Four 'overlapping' study areas—Integral Evolutionary Design, Aesthetic Evolutionary Design, Artificial Life-based Evolutionary Design, and Aesthetic Evolutionary AL—are the focus of this paper. All of these fields of study and their interconnections are illustrated in Figure 2.

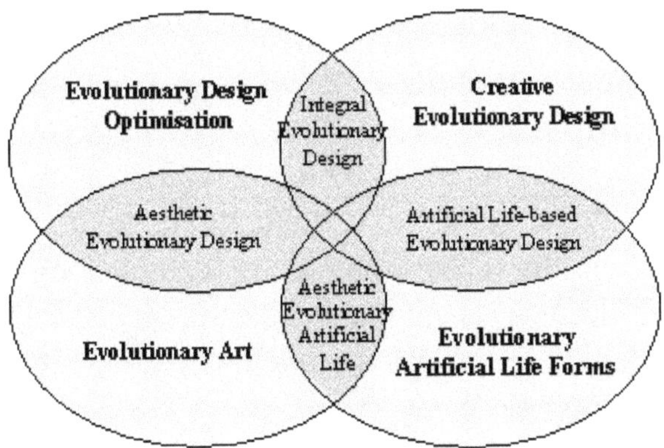

Source: - (Bentley, 2024)

Following this, we will examine the most important developments in each field of study, provide a high-level summary of the scope of research in each, and discuss the usual aims and purposes of scholars in each. For every part of Evolutionary Design, we give specific instances of its representations, evolutionary procedures, and evolved solutions. We wrap up by discussing some of the most typical problems and their solutions encountered by Evolutionary Design system developers.

20. *Representation and Encoding*

Data Representation: Encoding Information for Digital Processing

The complex procedure of data representation involves encoding and arranging information in a way that computer systems can efficiently store, transmit, and process. Data normalisation is the process of converting unstructured data into a form that computers can understand and work with. In order for computers to successfully understand, analyse, and manipulate data, a solid grasp of data representation is essential.

Data Representation

- **Binary Digits (Bits):** Standardized format representing data.

- **Numeric Formats**: Numeric, text, and multimedia formats facilitate interpretation and manipulation.

- **Character Encoding:** Translating Text into Binary.

- **Image, Audio, and Video Representation:** Multifaceted Data Structures

Binary Representation

Binary representation is fundamental to digital computing. Binary numbers, often known as bits, can take on the values 0 or 1 and are used by computers for storing and processing data. A computer system relies on bits as its basic data unit, which allow it to encode increasingly complex information. Computer systems rely on binary representation for storing, processing, and communicating data.

Source: - (bgiservice, 2024)

Numeric Representation: Numeric Representation:

Binary encoding systems are used for numerical data, which includes integers, floating-point numbers, and real numbers. An example of this is the use of fixed-width binary digits to represent integers, where each digit represents a power of two. The mantissa and the exponent work together to make floating-point numbers, which contain fractional parts, look like real numbers. A variety of numerical representation formats are available to meet the needs of different ranges, levels of precision, and processing demands, making numerical data handling quite versatile.

Source: - (bgiservice, 2024)

<u>**Character Encoding**</u>**:**

Symbols, text, and characters are encoded using systems like Unicode and ASCII. Computers can process text across languages and character sets thanks to these schemes that assign unique numerical codes to characters and symbols. The vast Unicode standard supports millions of letters and symbols, allowing for the smooth rendering of text in a variety of language situations.

Source: - (bgiservice, 2024)

Image, Audio, and Video Representation:

Images, audio, and video all have their own distinct representational formats that are specific to them, in addition to textual data. Many image formats exist, each having its own unique set of advantages and disadvantages when it comes to compression efficiency and image quality. Some examples of these formats are GIF, BMP, JPEG, and PNG. Just like how digital formats like WAV, MP3, AAC, and MP4 use compression techniques to keep quality while reducing file size, audio and video data do the same.

Source: - (bgiservice, 2024)

The term "data representation" refers to an umbrella term that covers a variety of formats and methods used to encode and organise data in computer systems. Data representation paves the way for contemporary computing by standardising data formats and encoding strategies, which in turn allow for the easy storage, transport, processing, and interpretation of information in digital settings.

20.1. Binary and Real-valued Encoding

SBE, or FIX Simple Binary Encoding, is aimed at trading systems that achieve high performance. Its design prioritises minimal bandwidth use and low encoding and decoding latency. Its intended purpose is to embody all FIX semantics in order to ensure compatibility.

This document lays out the technique for transmitting messages across wires. In this way, it facilitates communication by setting a baseline for interoperability. The standard is designed to be easily implementable, so users can tailor it to their own requirements. Implementers can use the most up-to-date idioms and techniques from computer languages to get data off the wire and manipulate it in applications.

Binary type system

Every field type that has been documented is supported so that typical FIX semantics can continue to work. Rather than using printable character representations of tag-value encoding, the type system relies on native binary data types and creates derived kinds as necessary.

The binary type system has been enhanced in these ways:

- Offers a way to define acceptable ranges of values and the precision of timestamps and decimal integers.

- Tells strings of varying lengths apart from character arrays of a set length. Gives you the option to set the string length that an app can handle.

- Enumerations, Boolean switches, and multiple-choice fields are organised in a consistent framework.

Design principles

Direct data access, free of complicated transformations and conditional logic, is the goal of the message design. This is achieved by:

- Simple kinds generated from native binaries, like prices and timestamps, as well as native binary data types, are used.

- Supporting immediate access to data and reducing the need to manage heaps of elements with varying lengths that must be progressively processed, fixed positions and fields with constant lengths are preferred.

Message schema

The standard lays forth the framework for messages and how fields are encoded. A message schema defines the format and contents of a certain message type. A message schema describes the fields that make up a message and where they are located inside the message. Metadata also specifies acceptable ranges of values and data that is not required to be transmitted over the wire, like constant values. Message schemas can be tailored to meet the individual needs of each counterparty or can be based on the standard FIX message standards.

<u>Glossary</u>

- **Character set** – A mapping between a sequence of octets and a sequence of characters.

- **Data type** – The encoding properties of a field type, such as the primitive types used for backing and the range of allowed values. The epoch of a date is one example of a type that has extra properties.

- **Encoding** – the structure of messages for communication. The most common application of the phrase is to describe the process of changing the format of data, such as text to binary. Nonetheless, SBE aspires to employ native binary data types to render conversion either unnecessary or trivial. In contrast to decoding, encoding also means arranging the structure of a message.

- **Message schema** – information about messages, including the kinds of data they contain and unique identifiers. Schemas for messages can be shared outside of the normal channel. Simultaneous Binary Encoding message formats are expressed in XML documents that adhere to an XML schema that was provided with this standard.

- **Message template** – description of data that identifies the fields of a specific message type. The schema of a message contains its template.

- **Session protocol** – message reliability throughout transport is the focus of this protocol. The message payload encoding process and the session protocol are two separate aspects of the FIX protocol. To check which protocols are compatible, visit the FIX protocol website and look at the specifications section. The FIX session protocol was originally called FIXT.

<u>Documentation</u>

This document explains:

- A field encoding method based on binary types

- The format of the message, which may include the following: the order of fields, groups of repeating elements, and any connections to a message header that the session protocol may supply.

- The Simplified Binary Coding message structure.

20.2. Permutation-based Encoding

Permutation encoding can be used in ordering problems, such as travelling salesman problem or task ordering problem.

In **permutation encoding**, every chromosome is a string of numbers that represent a position in a **sequence**.

Chromosome A	1 5 3 2 6 4 7 9 8
Chromosome B	8 5 6 7 2 3 1 4 9

Permutation encoding is useful for ordering problems. For some types of crossover and mutation corrections must be made to leave the chromosome consistent (i.e. have real sequence in it) for some problems.

Permutation-based encoding is a feature transformation approach that converts categorical data or sequences to numerical representation for machine learning models. It entails rearranging or permuting the elements of a categorical feature in order to encode significant patterns for algorithms to interpret and learn from the data. The basic idea is that by permuting the categorical variables, the relative relationships between the values are preserved, which can lead to improved model representation and predictive power, especially in cases where standard encoding techniques (such as one-hot or label encoding) may not fully capture the complexities of the feature relationships.

<u>Key Concepts:</u>

- **Handling Categorical Variables**: In machine learning, models often demand numerical input, therefore categorical variables must be converted into a format that algorithms can understand. Permutation-based encoding solves this problem by converting category data into numerical representations. It varies from traditional encoding methods such as one-hot encoding, which generates sparse matrices and may cause high-dimensionality concerns. Instead, permutation encoding gives a compact, ordered representation of the data, which can lead to more efficient and accurate learning.

- **Encoding Relationships**: A benefit of permutation-based encoding is that it may preserve the natural connections between categories. Using ordinal categorical data as an example, permutation encoding may represent the relative ordering of the values since categories have a natural order. Model performance is greatly affected by the correlations between categorical values; techniques like as decision trees, random forests, and gradient-boosted machines take this into consideration.

21. Selection Mechanisms

There are three different types of selection that are observed in nature:

Directional Selection

Source: - (Adams, 2023)

Directional Selection, individuals who possess 'outlying' traits – or traits that deviate significantly from the norm or average – have higher survivability and are therefore 'favored'.

How the peppered moth evolved in England during the 18th and 19th centuries is a good illustration of directional selection at action. The peppered moth used to be a lighter shade (the circle in the bottom left corner of the picture) before this. The mottling helped the moth blend in with the bark of the light-colored tree. That is why predators couldn't see them. Everything, even tree trunks, became darker as a result of the Industrial Revolution's soot pouring into the air. Soot had caked upon the trees. The peppered moth, which was light-colored, became more noticeable to its predators in these conditions. Since light-colored moths were more easily consumed, their phenotypic declined as a result. Those moths with the darker colour phenotypic made it through the season and even had offspring (circle on the top right of the picture). This means that the 'outlying' darker phenotype will likely increase in frequency as time goes on.

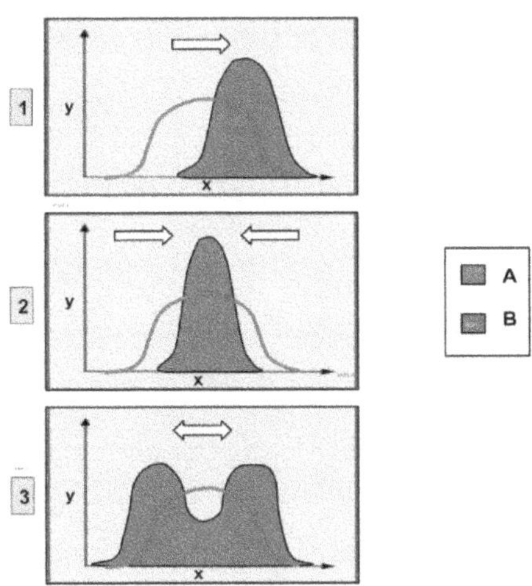

Source: - (Adams, 2023)

You can see directional selection in action in this graph. The phenotypic distribution in the initial population is depicted by the red line. The blue bell-shaped curve shows the affected population along a single axis.

Stabilizing Selection

Stabilising selection works by excluding outliers, or people who don't fit the mould.

Source: - (Adams, 2023)

The amount of eggs laid by robins provides a good illustration of stabilising selection in action. A robin typically lays clutches of four eggs. Because there needs to be more food for more chicks, the risk of malnutrition increases if more are produced. There may not be any healthy progeny if the egg number is too low. Consequently, the frequency of both big and small numbers of eggs will decrease, and only a fixed number, often the average, will be able to survive. As a result, there is less variation and the population "stabilises" around the mean, which in this example is three eggs.

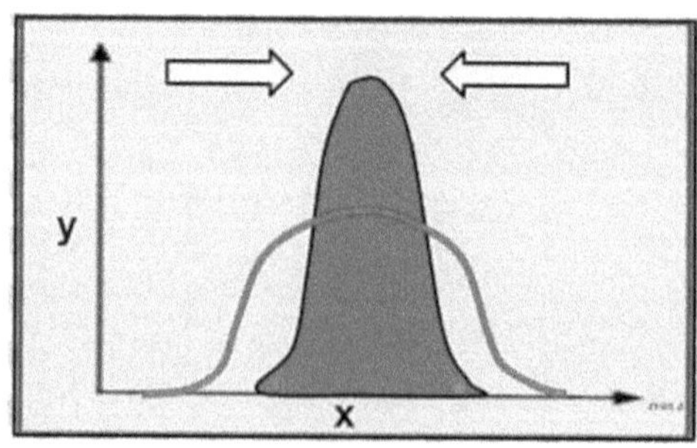

Source: - (Adams, 2023)

You can see stabilising selection in action in this graph. The initial population's distribution is depicted by the red line. There has been less variation in the stabilised population, as shown by the blue bell-shaped curve.

Disruptive Selection

The intermediate type may not always be the best option in a population when two or more different phenotypes exist. Here, the intermediate type is disturbed and has a lower chance of survival.

A group of rabbits residing in an area with a lot of rocks would be an illustration of disruptive selection in action. Unlike white rabbits, rabbits of the Himalayan or grey variety would blend in with the rocky terrain. Because predators could see them, the white rabbit population would gradually decline.

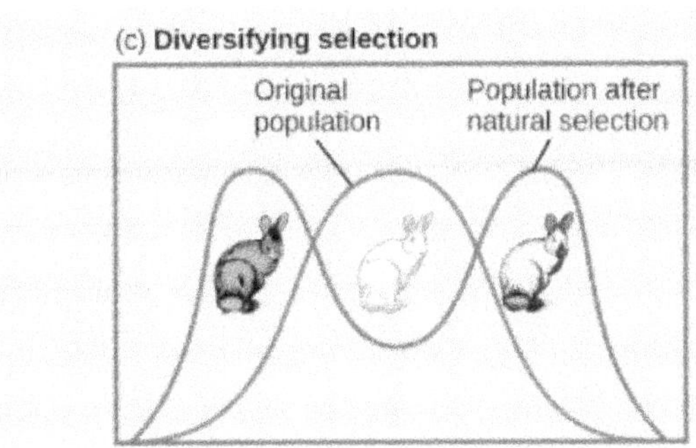

Source: - (Adams, 2023)

Above, you can see a graph showing disruptive selection in action. While the usual phenotype would go down, the number of lower and higher phenotypes would go up. Two separate populations may emerge as a result of this. Although there were a small number of black rabbits and white rabbits with black markings in the original population, the blue line shows that the majority of the rabbits were white. The affected population is shown by the red curve with two peaks. There is now more variation; for example, rabbits are more likely to be partially white or partially black than completely white.

21.1. Roulette Wheel Selection

Choosing at random from a set of weighted inputs is possible using a technique called roulette wheel selection, which is also called fitness-proportion selection.

This is done similarly to having a roulette wheel with all the desired inputs and only selecting an input based on the spin result.

How roulette wheel selection works

When spinning a standard roulette wheel, each result has the same chance of occurring. In roulette wheel selection, however, each result is weighted such that some are more likely to occur than others.

Balls are selected using a ticker, which spins before randomly stopping somewhere on the wheel.

For example, let's model picking a random colored ball from a bag with a weighted roulette wheel. For our example, we use:

- Five red balls

- Three blue balls

- Two orange balls

- One green ball

- Six yellow balls

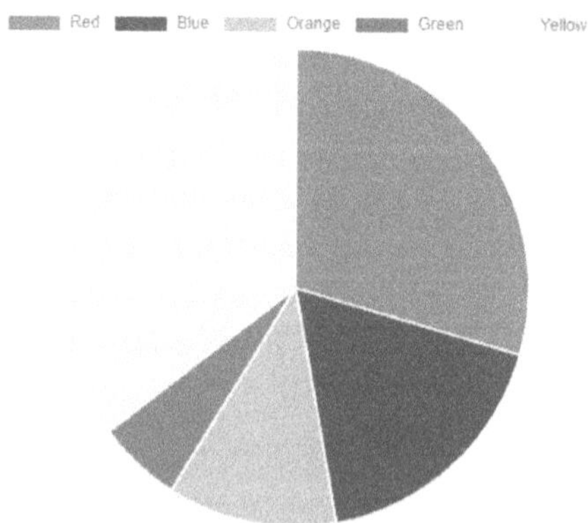

Source: - (Mohan, 2022)

We're always more likely to get the color red by spinning this roulette wheel. That is, any random ball we pick is more likely to be red. However, that doesn't mean we can't pick a color like green; it just has less probability of being selected.

Roulette wheel selection implementation

Explanation

- **Line 1:** We're just importing one useful function from the random module. We'll use this later.

- **Line 2–3:** We'll initialize two lists. One list has every color; the other has its number of occurrences or frequency.

- **Line 4:** We define and name our function, passing in inputs.

- **Line 5:** Create a variable called total_count. Inside this variable, we store the sum of all our inputs.

- **Line 6:** We'll find the probability of drawing any single colour of the ball. We iterate through our input, then divide each entry by the total number of entries in our input. Finally, we append our result to a new list called probabilities. We round our answer to two decimal places with the in-built round function.

- **Line 8:** We'll initialize a variable called random Number. In it, we are storing a random value between 0 and our max weight. This is done through the uniform method in our imported random module. This way, we can simulate a spin of the wheel. Here, think of the value of random Number as a random area we chose on a roulette wheel.

- **Line 10–12:** We'll create a new list called cumulative probability. We store the first value of our probability list here. Then, we iterate through probability, adding each iteration to the most recent value added to cumulative probability and append it at the end.

- **Line 16–17:** We'll initialize two variables, choose and count. Choose will be used to obtain our result, while count will get us the colour of our result.

- **Line 18–23:** We iterate through probabilities, adding its values to our chosen variable. If the value of choose is greater than or equal to our random Number, we print out this value. This is our selection. Printing out the corresponding value in our colour list using count gives us the right colour.

- **Line 24:** We'll exit the loop since we already have our answer.

The benefits of roulette wheel selection

Roulette wheel selection is beneficial in situations where we want controlled randomness. Anything can happen, but not everything is equally likely to happen.

In practical applications, this is often used when selecting genes for genetic algorithms. Here, we need to select a random gene to use later, but not all genes are equally likely to be selected. To simulate this, we use roulette wheel selection.

21.2. Tournament Selection

In a genetic algorithm, the best candidates from the current generation are chosen using a selection strategy called tournament selection. The next generation receives these chosen individuals. As part of a K-way tournament selection, we choose k participants and then hold a tournament with them. There is a rigorous selection process that culminates in the transmission of only the healthiest individuals to subsequent generations. This is how we narrow down the field to a manageable size, and then we pass the baton to the next generation of competitors. The selection pressure, a probability estimate of a candidate's chance of participating in a tournament, is another parameter it has. Weak candidates have less of a shot at being chosen if the tournament field is bigger since they will have to fight with better ones. The GA's convergence rate is defined by the selection pressure parameter. The rate of convergence increases as the selection pressure increases. Regardless of the kind of selection pressure, GAs can find the best or almost best option. Even when fitness levels are negative, Tournament Selection can be applied.

```
Algorithm --
1.Select k individuals from the population and perform a tournament amongst
them
2.Select the best individual from the k individuals
3. Repeat process 1 and 2 until you have the desired amount of population
```

Take the following into account: a three-way tournament, a starting population with fitness scores, and a target population size of six. For a visual representation of how our first tournament will unfold, refer to the diagram; the participant with the highest fitness value will proceed to the subsequent round.

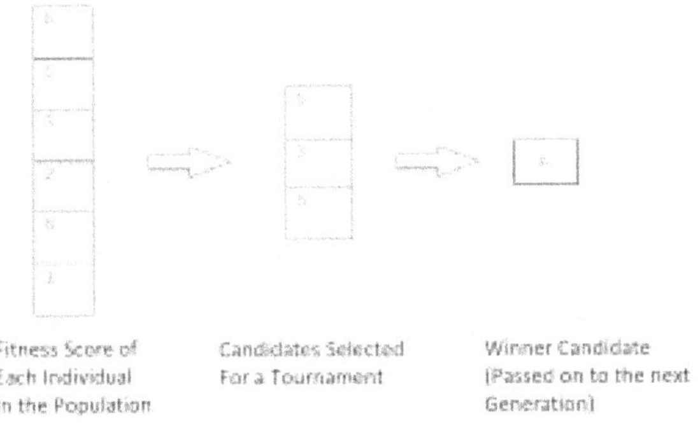

Source: - (GeeksforGeeks, 2018)

After the first tournament we have our selected population as.

We may be able to identify a representative sample after several of these competitions. In fact, it's possible. Therefore, the best chance of passing on a trait to the future generation lies with the strongest candidate. If we have a selection probability of p for the best candidate, then the likelihood of selecting the next best candidate is p*(1-p), and so on.

21.3. Rank-based Selection

Selecting chromosomes from the population to serve as crossover parents is something you are already familiar with from the GA outline. How to choose these chromosomes is the tricky part. The idea of evolution put out by Charles Darwin states that only the fittest should live to procreate. A number of approaches exist for choosing optimal chromosomes; these include, among others, the Boltzmann, tournament, rank, and steady state selection methods.

Roulette Wheel Selection

Physique is a determining factor in parent selection. The greater the likelihood of selection, the better the chromosomes. Picture this: the accompanying image is a representation of a genetic roulette wheel, with each chromosome given a large number corresponding to its fitness function.

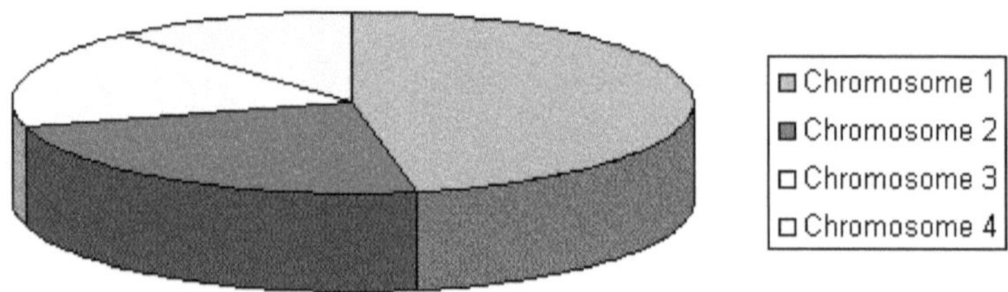

Source: - (Bennefall, 2016)

The next step is to choose the chromosome by dropping a marble there. More frequent selection will occur for chromosomes with higher fitness.

This can be simulated by following algorithm.

1. **[Sum]** Calculate sum of all chromosome fitnesses in population - sum S.

2. **[Select]** Generate random number from interval (0, S) - r.

3. **[Loop]** Go through the population and sum fitnesses from 0 - sum s. When the sum s is greater than r, stop and return the chromosome where you are.

Rank Selection

When there is a large difference in fitness, the prior selection will fail. As an illustration, consider a roulette wheel where the best chromosome fitness accounts for 90% of the total. In this case, the other chromosomes will have extremely slim possibilities of being chosen.

After sorting the population into a hierarchy, rank selection assigns fitness values to each chromosome. With fitness N (the total number of chromosomes in the population), the best will be at the top of the food chain, while the worst will be at the bottom.

Changing fitness to order number affects the situation, as you can see in the following picture.

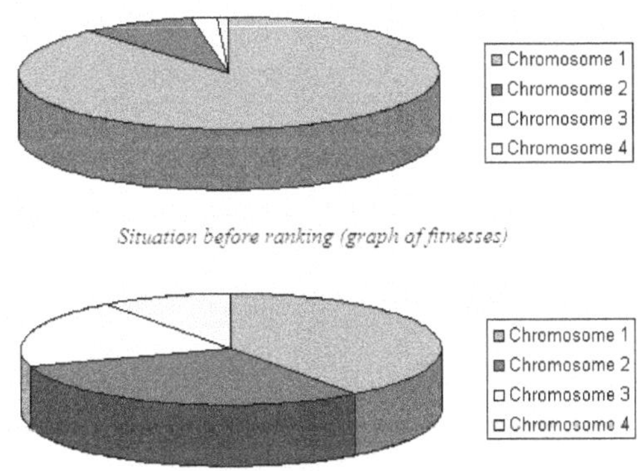

Situation before ranking (graph of fitnesses)

Situation after ranking (graph of order numbers)

Source: - (Bennefall, 2016)

Following this, every chromosome has an opportunity to be chosen. The top chromosomes don't differ significantly from the rest, therefore this approach might cause convergence to be slower.

<u>Steady-State Selection</u>

There is no specific way to choose parents using this strategy. A large number of chromosomes should make it to the next generation; this is the basic premise of natural selection.

GA operates in the subsequent manner. During each generation, a small number of chromosomes are chosen for reproduction based on their fitness level. Afterwards, a few chromosomes that aren't good for the future generation are taken out and replaced with others. Some people make it to the next generation.

Elitism

There has been prior introduction of the concept of elitism. There is a high probability that we will lose the best chromosome when we create new populations through mutation and crossover.

One approach, known as elitism, involves transferring only the best chromosomes (or a small number of exceptionally good ones) to a new population. All the other tasks are carried out using classical methods. Because it stops the best identified solution from being lost, elitism can drastically improve GA performance.

22. Crossover Operators

Crossover is a genetic operator used to vary the programming of a chromosome or chromosomes from one generation to the next. Crossover is sexual reproduction. Two strings are picked from the mating pool at random to crossover in order to produce superior offspring. The method chosen depends on the Encoding Method.

22.1. One-point and Multi-point Crossover

One Point Crossover

One-point crossover is used by the conventional genetic algorithm. This involves cutting the two mating chromosomes once at appropriate sites and then exchanging the sections that follow the cuts.

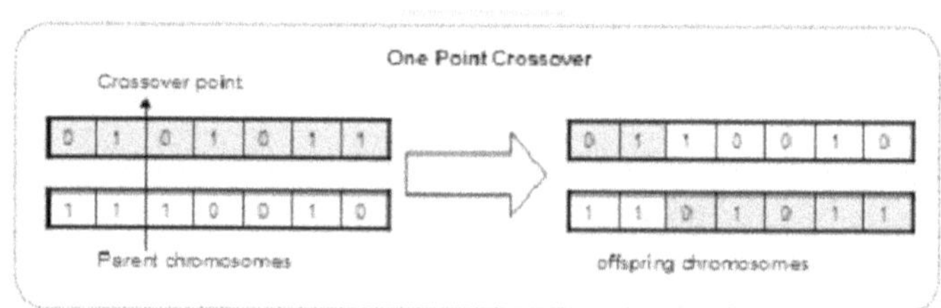

Source: - (GeeksforGeeks, 2019)

Two-point crossover

- Numerous crossover algorithms, frequently incorporating several cut points, have been developed in addition to single point crossover.

- Adding more crossover points lowers the GA's performance, so keep that in mind.

- More crossover points increase the likelihood of disruption to construction blocks, which is an issue.

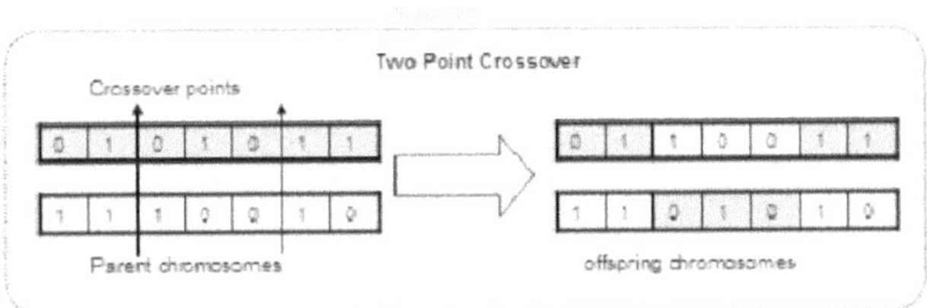

Source: - (GeeksforGeeks, 2019)

Multi-Point Crossover (N-Point crossover)

- Two-point crossover can potentially have the same issue as one point crossover.

- There is a way to apply this issue to every gene on a chromosome.

- The likelihood of passing on a set of genes from an N-points crossover increases when those genes are located close together on a chromosome.

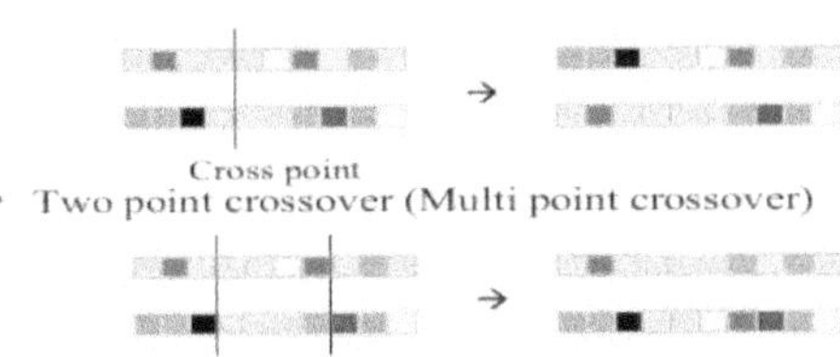

Source: - (GeeksforGeeks, 2019)

22.2. Uniform Crossover

There is a significant difference between the N-point crossover and uniform crossover. To produce a child with a specific set of genes, it is necessary to replicate those genes in both parents using a binary crossover mask that is both randomly generated and has the same length as the chromosomes.

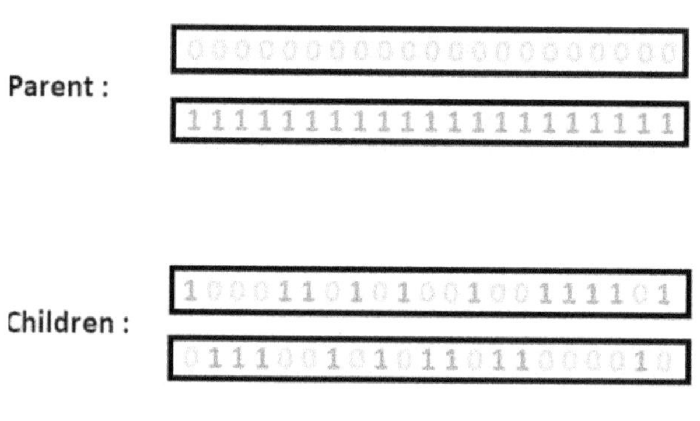

Uniform Crossover

Source: - (GeeksforGeeks, 2019)

<u>**Arithmetic Crossover**</u>

- Arithmetic Crossover Chromosomes having real value or floating-point representation

- undergo arithmetic crossover.

- This crossover creates a new allele at each gene position in the offspring.

- The value of new allele lies between the values of the parent alleles.

- The value of new alleles for offspring is computed using following equation:

- Offspring1 = w*parent1 + (1-w)*Parent2

- Offspring2= (1-w) *parent1 + w*Parent2

- Where w is constant weight factor that is used to compute new values.

23. Fitness Evaluation

Physical fitness is crucial to one's well-being. Preventing common ailments, such as cardiovascular disease, is a breeze when you exercise consistently according to your body's needs. How can one find out what their body needs most effectively? Come see us at Hoag Executive Health!

Our time- and space-saving comprehensive physicals include a fitness examination as one of their cornerstones.

Get Physical with Your Physical

As part of their comprehensive physical, those enrolled in Hoag Executive Health can anticipate to receive a full fitness exam. During the fitness exam, our exercise physiologists can identify the patient's strengths and areas that could use some development.

Source: - (Stokkebye, 2022)

Convenient, Time-Efficient Care

This all-encompassing evaluation makes use of cutting-edge equipment housed in our fitness centres to gauge not only cardiovascular fitness and muscular endurance (upper and lower body), but also injury prevention via measures like visual movement analysis and posture screening.

Why is getting a fitness evaluation important?

Examining your mobility is the crux of the fitness section. Our exercise physiologists can use this time to assess your current level of flexibility, strength, and cardiovascular reserve, as well as identify areas where you might improve to reduce the risk of injury. Finding the most effective means of assisting patients in reaching their fitness and performance goals is our top priority.

Your personal care team can use the results from the fitness portion to create a program specifically for you based on your needs, taking into account any compensating patterns in your movement. You may find that stretching and other remedial exercises become second nature if you start doing them regularly. Our exercise physiologists can advise you on pain-free and active desk exercises to do while you work long hours at a computer.

Reaching Peak Performance

While fitness is an often-overlooked aspect of standard physicals, it is vital to a person's health and can have far-reaching consequences if not addressed.

Everyone has different requirements, and we at Hoag Executive Health want to treat each patient as an individual. That is why we tailor our evaluation procedures to each client's specific requirements. For additional information, contact us at (949) 202-4923 right now and take charge of your health!

23.1. Objective Function Design

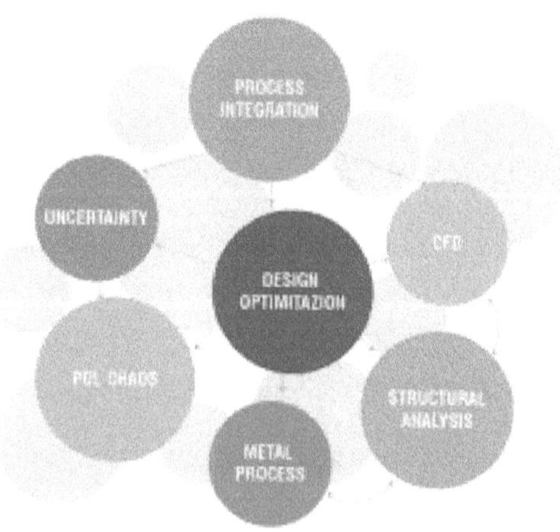

Source: - (Rathinam, 2024)

Optimization and design analysis

Optimization and design analysis in the context of the Finite Element Method (FEM) involve using numerical simulations to improve the design of a structure or system by optimizing certain parameters or performance metrics. Here's how optimization and design analysis can be conducted using FEM:

- **Problem Formulation:** The first step in optimization and design analysis is to clearly define the objectives and constraints of the problem. This includes specifying the design variables (e.g., geometry, material properties) that can be adjusted, as well as any constraints on these variables (e.g., manufacturing limitations, structural requirements).

- **Finite Element Modeling:** A finite element model of the system or structure of interest is created, incorporating the geometry, material properties, boundary conditions, and loading conditions. This model serves as the basis for performing numerical simulations using FEM.

- **Objective Function Definition:** An objective function is defined to quantify the performance of the design. This could be, for example, minimizing the weight of a structure subject to certain strength constraints, maximizing the efficiency of a heat exchanger, or minimizing the drag force on an aerodynamic component.

- **Design Variables and Constraints:** The design variables and constraints are incorporated into the optimization problem formulation. These variables represent the parameters that can be adjusted during the optimization process, while the constraints ensure that any proposed design satisfies certain requirements or limitations.

- **Optimization Algorithm:** An optimization algorithm is selected to search for the optimal solution to the design problem. This could be a gradient-based method (e.g., gradient descent, quasi-Newton methods) or a heuristic method (e.g., genetic algorithms, particle swarm optimization) depending on the complexity of the problem and the nature of the objective function and constraints.

- **Finite Element Analysis (FEA):** The optimization algorithm iteratively evaluates different designs by performing finite element analyses using FEM. Each analysis computes the performance metrics specified by the objective function and checks whether the design satisfies the imposed constraints.

- **Iterative Optimization:** The optimization algorithm iterates through a series of design evaluations, adjusting the design variables at each step to improve the objective function while satisfying the constraints. This process continues until a satisfactory design is found or until a stopping criterion is met.

- **Sensitivity Analysis:** Sensitivity analysis may be performed to assess the sensitivity of the optimal solution to changes in the design variables and to identify critical parameters that have a significant impact on the performance of the system.

- **Validation and Verification:** Once an optimal design is obtained, it is important to validate and verify the results using additional analyses, such as comparing against experimental data or performing robustness checks to ensure the reliability of the optimized solution.

- **Implementation and Documentation:** Finally, the optimized design is implemented and documented, including any necessary revisions to the original design specifications and a summary of the optimization process and results.

Optimization and design analysis using FEM allow engineers and designers to explore a wide range of design possibilities, identify optimal solutions, and improve the performance and efficiency of engineering systems and structures.

23.2. Evaluation Strategies and Constraints

Finding out what the program wants to learn is the first step in creating an evaluation. You can learn a lot about the program's execution by asking process evaluation questions. Program achievements and failures can also be found using them. The program's performance in meeting its objectives and the program's impact on participants, both in the short and long term, can be assessed using outcome evaluation questions. When formulating evaluation questions, program planners should think about the available data, what information program stakeholders would find useful, and how the results would be put to use.

Examples of process evaluation questions include:

- What did the organization accomplish during the reporting period?

- How many people were served?

- How many sessions were completed?

- What services were delivered?

- How did community members, participants, and staff perceive the program?

- How well did documentation systems capture program and participant data?

- What were the barriers and challenges that affected program implementation?

- Who facilitated the implementation of the program?

- What program activities were not completed and why? If activities changed, why did they change?

- What are key lessons learned?

Examples of outcome evaluation questions include:

- What were the outcomes of the program?

  o Did the program improve participants' ability to manage their health condition?

  o Did the program increase participants' likelihood to make lifestyle changes?

- ○ Did the program increase participants' compliance with their medications?

- ○ Did the program connect participants with a primary care physician/medical home?

- ○ Did the program improve participant quality of life?

- Did the program result in cost savings to the healthcare system?

- ○ What aspects of the program were most cost-effective or least cost-effective?

- Which outcomes are important to the community?

Evaluation Considerations

Community health worker (CHW) programs vary greatly, hence there isn't a universal method for assessing their effectiveness. Important factors to consider while assessing CHW programs are:

- **Staffing** – CHW programs have the option of using an outside firm or a member of their own team to conduct evaluations. It is possible to appoint CHWs to conduct surveys or gather data for program evaluations. Additional training may be necessary for CHWs to carry out these duties.

- **Cost-Effectiveness and Return on Investment** – Measuring the expenses of CHW programs can be crucial. Screening for cancer, diabetes, and cardiovascular disease are just a few of the illnesses for which the Community Preventive Services Task Force (CPSTF) has found that CHW interventions can be cost-effective. It is possible to prove the program's ROI with more thorough evaluations. Community partners may be ready to invest in a program's long-term viability if it can prove its efficacy with data on costs and return on investment (ROI). New evidence suggests that rural CHW programs can achieve their aims while remaining cost-effective.

- **Existing Gaps in Evidence** – The CPSTF has pointed out a number of areas where there is a lack of evidence. These include interventions that have a longer follow-up period (more than 12 months), interventions that target diverse subgroups of the population, the effects of large-scale interventions involving more than 500 people, and the relative effectiveness of face-to-face, telephone, and group service delivery on outcomes.

24. Chapter Summary

This chapter covers the essential components of evolutionary algorithms, focusing on representation and encoding, selection mechanisms, crossover and mutation operators, and fitness evaluation.

In representation and encoding, different methods are used to represent solutions. Binary encoding uses strings of 0s and 1s, while real-valued encoding represents solutions as real numbers, often used in continuous optimization. Permutation-based encoding is useful for problems like the traveling salesman, where the order of elements is crucial.

Selection mechanisms determine how individuals are chosen for reproduction. Roulette wheel selection uses a probability proportional to fitness, while tournament selection pits individuals against each other in small groups. Rank-based selection ranks individuals by fitness, ensuring diversity by reducing the probability of selecting only the fittest.

In crossover operators, solutions combine information from two parents. One-point and multi-point crossover divide parent strings and swap sections, while uniform crossover randomly exchanges genes between parents, increasing genetic diversity.

Mutation operators introduce random variations. Bit-flip mutation changes binary-encoded solutions by flipping bits, and Gaussian mutation adds random noise to real-valued solutions, helping maintain diversity and avoid premature convergence.

Fitness evaluation measures the quality of solutions. Designing an appropriate objective function is critical, as it guides the algorithm toward optimal solutions. Evaluation strategies may include penalty functions for constraint violations, ensuring that solutions respect problem-specific limits.

Part 1: (Very Short Questions)

1. What is binary encoding in genetic algorithms?

2. How does real-valued encoding differ from binary encoding?

3. What is permutation-based encoding used for?

4. How does roulette wheel selection work in genetic algorithms?

5. What is tournament selection, and how is it applied?

6. What is the purpose of rank-based selection?

7. How does one-point crossover differ from multi-point crossover?

8. What is uniform crossover in genetic algorithms?

9. What is bit-flip mutation, and when is it used?

10. How does Gaussian mutation modify real-valued genes?

Part 2: (Short Questions)

1. What is the difference between binary encoding and real-valued encoding in genetic algorithms?

2. How does tournament selection differ from roulette wheel selection?

3. What is the purpose of one-point and multi-point crossover in genetic algorithms?

4. How does a bit-flip mutation work compared to a Gaussian mutation?

5. What factors should be considered when designing an objective function for fitness evaluation in genetic algorithms?

Part 3: (Long Questions)

1. What are the differences between binary and real-valued encoding in genetic algorithms, and how do these encoding methods impact the performance and suitability of algorithms in solving optimization problems? Provide examples of situations where one type of encoding may be preferred over the other.

2. How do Roulette Wheel Selection, Tournament Selection, and Rank-based Selection mechanisms differ in genetic algorithms, and what are the key advantages and disadvantages of each method in terms of solution diversity and convergence rates?

3. What are the key differences between One-point, Multi-point, and Uniform Crossover operators in genetic algorithms, and how do these crossover methods affect the exploration and exploitation of the search space? In what scenarios would one method be more effective than the others?

4. How do Bit-flip Mutation and Gaussian Mutation operators function in genetic algorithms, and what are their respective roles in maintaining genetic diversity? How can mutation rates be controlled to prevent premature convergence while still promoting an effective search process?

5. Why is the design of the objective function crucial in the fitness evaluation of genetic algorithms, and how do evaluation strategies and constraints influence the algorithm's performance? Provide examples where fitness evaluation plays a critical role in obtaining optimal solutions.

Part 4: (MCQs)

1. Which of the following is a characteristic of binary encoding?

   a. Uses floating-point numbers to represent solutions

   b. Uses discrete values (0s and 1s) to represent solutions

   c. Uses a sequence of real numbers to represent solutions

   d. Uses permutations to represent solutions

2. In real-valued encoding, how are solutions represented?

   a. As a sequence of 0s and 1s

   b. As permutations of elements

   c. As real numbers within a continuous range

   d. As integers only

3. Which selection mechanism gives higher chances of selection to individuals with a higher fitness value?

    a. Tournament Selection

    b. Rank-based Selection

    c. Roulette Wheel Selection

    d. Random Selection

4. What happens during tournament selection in genetic algorithms?

    a. All individuals have an equal probability of selection

    b. A subset of individuals is randomly selected, and the best one is chosen

    c. Individuals are selected based on their rank in the population

    d. Crossover is applied before selection

5. What is a key feature of rank-based selection in genetic algorithms?

    a. Fitness values directly influence the probability of selection

    b. Individuals are selected based on their position in a sorted list

    c. It involves a tournament of multiple individuals

    d. Random selection is used to rank individuals

6. Which crossover operator involves splitting the parent chromosomes at a single random point and swapping the segments?

    a. Uniform Crossover

    b. Multi-point Crossover

    c. One-point Crossover

    d. Arithmetic Crossover

7. In uniform crossover, how is the offspring generated?

   a. By copying segments from each parent at multiple random points

   b. By exchanging corresponding genes between parents based on a fixed crossover point

   c. By randomly choosing each gene from one of the parents

   d. By splitting parents at two or more points and combining segments

8. What is the role of mutation in genetic algorithms?

   a. To select the fittest individuals for crossover

   b. To introduce diversity by altering some genes in the offspring

   c. To evaluate the fitness of solutions

   d. To ensure the elimination of weak individuals

9. Which mutation operator is commonly used for binary encoding?

   a. Gaussian Mutation

   b. Real-value Mutation

   c. Bit-flip Mutation

   d. Uniform Mutation

10. In fitness evaluation, what is typically used to measure how good a solution is?

    a. Objective function

    b. Selection operator

    c. Crossover operator

    d. Mutation rate

Answer

1	2	3	4	5	6	7	8	9	10
b	c	c	b	b	c	c	b	c	a

CHAPTER 5

ADAPTIVE AND HYBRID APPROACHES

25. Introduction

Many industrial processes, particularly manufacturing systems, rely heavily on the concepts of process scheduling and process planning. Process planning is a tool used in this area to map out the various stages of manufacturing in accordance with product requirements. In addition, the scheduling idea establishes the process plan's guidelines for the utilisation of resources. Conventional and rudimentary optimisation techniques often approach this issue sequentially. Conversely, hybrid approaches that include process planning and scheduling are gaining popularity as processor computing capacities rise(Moon et al., 2008).

No known algorithm can accurately solve many scheduling issues with real-world applications in polynomial time. The P complexity level does not cover such issues. Consequently, metaheuristic algorithms have been the go-to for actual scheduling difficulties in industries since the 1970s. The Genetic Algorithm (GA) and its hybrid variants are extensively utilised in integrated scheduling and planning systems due to their popularity as optimisation methodologies. The process is based on evolution through natural selection. An additional approach for minimising maximum completion in Integrated Process Planning and Scheduling (IPPS) problems is Ant Colony Optimisation (ACO). The ant's strategy for finding food in a network served as inspiration for this time-based optimisation method based on mutation and crossover mechanisms(Cifci, 2023).

There are a number of theoretical and experimental investigations published in this area. Presented below, in chronological order, are a number of noteworthy research. Initially, Allahverdi and Aldowaisan introduced various novel heuristic algorithms for multi-machine non-waiting flow-type problems that consider the total completion time. They demonstrated that these algorithms outperform existing methods, including the recently created GA, in terms of error performance.

A hybrid GA, proposed by Tseng and Lin, can resolve completion-time-oriented scheduling issues of the non-wait flow kind. The offered technique integrates GA with a novel local search scheme. Insertion Search and Cut-and-Repair techniques are combined in the local search algorithm.

Not one, but two data mining methods have been investigated by the Li et al. study team. Here, the approaches utilised include artificial neural networks and binary logistic regression. Their approach was evaluated in comparison to the suggested graphically-based hyper-intuitive solutions for test scheduling problems. The time complexity analysis revealed that the research may be completed more quickly with the help of artificial neural networks and the binary logistic regression method. Their assistance has allowed for the development of decision support systems that rely on information. In their pursuit of the fastest possible execution time, Araujo and Nagano have looked into scheduling issues. Although it only contributed a minor contribution, this problem is well-known for being NP-hard. Their research led to the development of GAP Heuristics with a structural property base, a novel constructive heuristic approach. Both the intuitive TRIPS (Triple) proposed by Brown, McGarvey, and Ventura and the well-known TWOs proposed by Bianco, Dell'Olmo, and Giordani form the basis of the suggested methodology. The latter two methods are more efficient in terms of the amount of time needed to run the computations(Alizadeh Foroutan et al., 2023)

26. *Adaptive Evolutionary Computation*

Among the many subfields of evolutionary computation (EC), one that deals with optimisation and problem environment changes is known as adaptive evolutionary computation (AEC). Because of its flexibility, the algorithm is better able to deal with unpredictable and ever-changing situations than more conventional evolutionary methods.

<u>**Key Concepts of Adaptive Evolutionary Computation**</u>:

1. **Evolutionary Computation (EC):** Algorithms in evolutionary computing (EC) draw inspiration from biological evolution and constitute a branch of AI and optimisation. Methods like selection, mutation, recombination, and inheritance are employed by these algorithms to gradually evolve solutions to optimisation issues. Some examples of EC approaches are Differential Evolution (DE), Evolution Strategies (ES), Genetic Algorithms (GA), and Genetic Programming (GP).

2. **Adaptation in EC:** Many parameters (such as the population size, mutation rate, and crossover rate) in conventional evolutionary algorithms are often held constant during the run. But adaptive EC makes real-time changes to these settings in response to optimisation or environmental feedback. Modifying mutation rates in reaction to stagnation, selection pressure, or crossover rates is one way to achieve this.

3. **Dynamic Environments:** Adaptive evolutionary computation is particularly useful in dynamic or uncertain environments where the optimization landscape changes over time. These could be environments where the objective function or constraints are not static but change periodically or unpredictably.

4. **Self-Adaptive Mechanisms:** Many AEC algorithms incorporate self-adaptive mechanisms where parameters controlling the evolutionary process evolve alongside the solutions. For instance, in self-adaptive Differential Evolution, both the problem solutions and the parameters governing the evolution

(e.g., crossover rate) are encoded in the chromosome and evolved together.

5. **Multi-Objective Optimization:** AEC is also applied to multi-objective optimization problems, where it needs to adapt to conflicting objectives and maintain diversity among solutions to explore the trade-offs effectively.

6. **Real-World Applications:** Adaptive evolutionary algorithms have been applied in fields such as robotics, control systems, finance, engineering design, and bioinformatics, where adaptability to changing conditions is crucial.

Examples of Adaptive Mechanisms in Evolutionary Computation:

- **Adaptive Mutation Rate:** The mutation rate may increase if the population converges too quickly, or it may decrease when the population is sufficiently diverse.

- **Variable Population Size:** The size of the population may change dynamically based on the progress of the optimization process.

- **Adaptive Selection Pressure:** The intensity of selection may vary depending on how the population evolves, with a stronger selection pressure in early stages and a relaxed one later on.

Challenges:

- **Balancing Adaptation:** Over-adaptation can lead to premature convergence or loss of diversity, while under-adaptation may slow down the optimization process.

- **Complexity:** Introducing adaptive mechanisms increases the complexity of the algorithm, which can make analysis and tuning more challenging.

Overall, adaptive evolutionary computation represents a powerful enhancement to traditional evolutionary algorithms, making them more flexible and capable of handling a wide range of dynamic and complex optimization problems.

26.1. Self-adaptive Parameters

Self-adaptive parameters refer to a strategy used primarily in optimization algorithms where the parameters of the algorithm dynamically adjust themselves during the optimization process, rather than being set manually by the user. This technique is especially common in evolutionary algorithms, metaheuristic methods, and machine learning models to improve performance, reduce the need for parameter tuning, and enhance generalization(Li et al., 2013).

<u>**Key Concepts:**</u>

1. **Evolutionary Algorithms:**

   - In evolutionary algorithms (EAs) such as Genetic Algorithms (GAs), Differential Evolution (DE), and Evolution Strategies (ES), self-adaptive parameters refer to parameters like mutation rate, crossover rate, and step size that evolve along with the solutions.

   - The parameters are encoded into the individual solutions (genomes), and through the process of selection, crossover, and mutation, the parameters adapt to the search space and the problem being solved.

   - Example: Example: In Differential Evolution, the mutation factor F and crossover rate CR can be encoded in the individual genomes and allowed to evolve, resulting in adaptive control of exploration and exploitation.

2. **Metaheuristic Methods:**

   - Self-adaptation is used in other metaheuristic algorithms like Particle Swarm Optimization (PSO), Ant Colony Optimization (ACO), and Simulated Annealing.

   - For instance, in PSO, the inertia weight, which controls the exploration and exploitation trade-off, can be self-adaptive, changing dynamically based on the swarm's performance.

3. **Machine Learning**

- In some machine learning algorithms, self-adaptive parameters can refer to the automatic adjustment of learning rates, regularization strengths, or hyperparameters during training.

- Algorithms like Adam or AdaGrad can be seen as self-adaptive methods for learning rates in neural network training.

4. **Self-adaptive Control:**

- A broader interpretation includes adaptive control systems in fields like robotics, where the control parameters of the system adjust in real-time based on the system's performance and environment(Li et al., 2013).

Benefits:

- Reduced Manual Tuning: Self-adaptive parameters reduce the need for extensive manual tuning, which can be time-consuming and problem-specific.

- Dynamic Adjustment: These parameters adjust dynamically based on the search space, which can lead to faster convergence and better solutions.

- Improved Robustness: Self-adaptation can make algorithms more robust to varying problem landscapes by continuously adjusting to optimize performance.

Challenges:

- Complexity: Introducing self-adaptive parameters can increase the complexity of the algorithm.

- Convergence Issues: If not properly managed, self-adaptive parameters might lead to premature convergence or excessive exploration.

Example:

In Differential Evolution (DE), self-adaptive DE might allow the mutation factor F and rossover rate CR to evolve along with the population, rather than being fixed. The individuals in the population carry these parameters as part of their genomes, and through selection, better-performing individuals with well-suited parameters propagate, leading to an adaptive optimization process.

Self-adaptive parameters represent an advanced strategy in algorithm design, particularly suited for problems where the optimal settings for parameters are not known a priori and may change as the algorithm progresses.

26.2. Adaptive Mutation and Crossover Rates

Adaptive mutation and crossover rates are techniques used in evolutionary algorithms to improve their performance by dynamically adjusting these key parameters during the search process. Mutation and crossover are critical operators in genetic algorithms and related methods, influencing exploration (diversity) and exploitation (convergence) in the search space. Adapting these rates allows the algorithm to fine-tune its behavior based on the progress of the search, leading to more effective optimization(Spears, 1998).

<u>Concepts:</u>

1. **Mutation Rate:**

   The mutation rate determines how often random changes are introduced into the population. In genetic algorithms, this typically involves altering genes in a solution (individual) to introduce new genetic material.

   Exploration: A higher mutation rate encourages more exploration by introducing diverse solutions.

   Exploitation: A lower mutation rate favors exploitation, allowing the algorithm to refine and converge on good solutions.

   Adaptive mutation rates adjust based on the algorithm's progress—e.g., increasing mutation when diversity is low and reducing it as the population converges.

2. **Crossover Rate:**

The crossover rate controls how often crossover (recombination of genetic material from two parents) occurs to create offspring.

Exploration: A higher crossover rate enhances exploration by mixing genes from different parents, leading to potentially novel solutions.

Exploitation: A lower crossover rate promotes exploitation by preserving existing high-quality solutions.

Adaptive crossover rates adjust to balance exploration and exploitation throughout the algorithm's run.

<u>Adaptive Strategies:</u>

1. **Feedback-Based Adaptation:**

   - Mutation and crossover rates are adapted based on the feedback from the population's performance. If the population is stagnating, the algorithm may increase the mutation rate to introduce diversity. Conversely, if the population is making good progress, the mutation rate might be reduced to focus on fine-tuning solutions.

   - **Example:** In Differential Evolution (DE), adaptive strategies can modify the crossover rate and mutation factor based on the success of recent generations. Parameters that contribute to successful offspring are favored.

2. **Self-Adaptive Parameters:**

   - In self-adaptive strategies, each individual in the population carries its own mutation and crossover rates as part of its genetic representation. These rates evolve alongside the solution itself.

   - Successful individuals with effective mutation and crossover rates pass those rates on to the next generation, allowing the rates to evolve naturally.

- **Example:** In self-adaptive DE or Evolution Strategies (ES), the mutation and crossover rates are encoded into the individual genomes, and their evolution is governed by the algorithm's selection process.

3. **Time-Varying Parameters:**

   - Another adaptive approach is to vary the mutation and crossover rates according to a pre-defined schedule. For example, starting with high mutation and crossover rates to explore the search space broadly, then gradually decreasing them to refine solutions as the algorithm progresses(Lin et al., 2003).

   - **Example:** In a Genetic Algorithm, the mutation rate might start high and decrease linearly over time as the population converges toward an optimal solution.

4. **Fitness-Based Adaptation:**

   - Mutation and crossover rates are adjusted based on the fitness of the individuals in the population. If individuals are close to optimal fitness, the algorithm might reduce mutation and crossover rates to focus on local exploitation. Conversely, if fitness improvements are stagnating, the rates might increase to explore new areas of the search space.

Benefits of Adaptive Mutation and Crossover:

- **Improved Convergence:** By dynamically adjusting mutation and crossover rates, the algorithm can avoid premature convergence and improve the quality of the final solution.

- **Better Exploration and Exploitation:** Adaptive rates balance the exploration of new solutions with the exploitation of known good solutions, which can lead to more effective optimization.

- **Reduced Sensitivity to Hyperparameters:** Traditional algorithms require careful tuning of fixed mutation and crossover rates. Adaptive strategies reduce the sensitivity to these settings by allowing the algorithm to adjust them automatically.

Challenges:

- **Complexity:** Introducing adaptive mechanisms increases the complexity of the algorithm, as the rules governing adaptation need to be carefully designed.

- **Overhead:** Tracking and adjusting parameters dynamically adds computational overhead, which may slow down the algorithm in some cases.

- **Parameter Control:** While adaptation can improve performance, poorly designed adaptation rules might lead to suboptimal behavior, such as too much exploration or too rapid convergence.

Example in Practice:

In Genetic Algorithms (GA), an adaptive mutation rate might work as follows:

- **Initial Phase:** The mutation rate is set high to allow for broad exploration of the search space.

- **Middle Phase:** As the population begin

- Middle Phase: As the population begins to converge, the mutation rate is gradually reduced to allow for more focused exploitation of good solutions.

- **Stagnation Detection:** If the algorithm detects that the population is stagnating (e.g., no significant improvement in fitness over several generations), it can temporarily increase the mutation rate to reintroduce diversity and explore new areas of the search space.

Algorithms become more resilient and adaptable across a variety of problem landscapes when they are able to adapt their mutation and crossover rates to the optimisation challenge at hand.

27. *Hybrid Algorithms*

Adaptive mutation and crossover rates are techniques used in evolutionary algorithms to improve their performance by dynamically adjusting these key parameters during the search process. Mutation and crossover are critical operators in genetic algorithms and related methods, influencing exploration (diversity) and exploitation (convergence) in the search space. Adapting these rates allows the algorithm to fine-tune its behavior based on the progress of the search, leading to more effective optimization(Sipper et al., 2018).

<u>Concepts:</u>

1. **Mutation Rate:**

   - The mutation rate determines how often random changes are introduced into the population. In genetic algorithms, this typically involves altering genes in a solution (individual) to introduce new genetic material.

   - Exploration: A higher mutation rate encourages more exploration by introducing diverse solutions.

   - Exploitation: A lower mutation rate favors exploitation, allowing the algorithm to refine and converge on good solutions.

   - Adaptive mutation rates adjust based on the algorithm's progress—e.g., increasing mutation when diversity is low and reducing it as the population converges.

2. **Crossover Rate:**

   - The crossover rate controls how often crossover (recombination of genetic material from two parents) occurs to create offspring.

   - Exploration: A higher crossover rate enhances exploration by mixing genes from different parents, leading to potentially novel solutions.

   - Exploitation: A lower crossover rate promotes exploitation by preserving existing high-quality solutions.

   - Adaptive crossover rates adjust to balance exploration and exploitation throughout the algorithm's run.

Adaptive Strategies:

1. Feedback-Based Adaptation:

- The population's performance feeds into the adjustment of mutation and crossover rates. If the population is stagnating, the algorithm may increase the mutation rate to introduce diversity. Conversely, if the population is making good progress, the mutation rate might be reduced to focus on fine-tuning solutions.

- Example: In Differential Evolution (DE), adaptive strategies can modify the crossover rate and mutation factor based on the success of recent generations. Parameters that contribute to successful offspring are favored.

2. Self-Adaptive Parameters:

- In self-adaptive strategies, each individual in the population carries its own mutation and crossover rates as part of its genetic representation. These rates evolve alongside the solution itself.

- Successful individuals with effective mutation and crossover rates pass those rates on to the next generation, allowing the rates to evolve naturally.

- Example: In self-adaptive DE or Evolution Strategies (ES), the mutation and crossover rates are encoded into the individual genomes, and their evolution is governed by the algorithm's selection process.

3. Time-Varying Parameters:

- Using a pre-established timetable to vary mutation and crossover rates is another adaptive strategy. As an example, the algorithm can begin by exploring the search space extensively with high mutation and crossover rates, and then it can gradually decrease them to refine solutions as it advances.

- Example: In a Genetic Algorithm, the mutation rate might start high and decrease linearly over time as the population converges toward an optimal solution.

4. **Fitness-Based Adaptation:**

Mutation and crossover rates are adjusted based on the fitness of the individuals in the population. If individuals are close to optimal fitness, the algorithm might reduce mutation and crossover rates to focus on local exploitation. Conversely, if fitness improvements are stagnating, the rates might increase to explore new areas of the search space(Gómez, 2023).

Benefits of Adaptive Mutation and Crossover:

- **Improved Convergence:** The technique is able to prevent early convergence and enhance the final solution quality by dynamically modifying mutation and crossover rates.

- **Better Exploration and Exploitation:** For better optimisation, adaptive rates should be used to balance the use of known good solutions with the investigation of new ones.

- **Reduced Sensitivity to Hyperparameters:** Traditional algorithms require careful tuning of fixed mutation and crossover rates. Adaptive strategies reduce the sensitivity to these settings by allowing the algorithm to adjust them automatically.

Challenges:

- Complexity: Introducing adaptive mechanisms increases the complexity of the algorithm, as the rules governing adaptation need to be carefully designed.

- Overhead: Tracking and adjusting parameters dynamically adds computational overhead, which may slow down the algorithm in some cases.

- Parameter Control: While adaptation can improve performance, poorly designed adaptation rules might lead to suboptimal behavior, such as too much exploration or too rapid convergence.

Example in Practice:

In Genetic Algorithms (GA), an adaptive mutation rate might work as follows:

- **Initial Phase:** The mutation rate is set high to allow for broad exploration of the search space.

- **Middle Phase:** As the population begins to converge, the mutation rate is gradually reduced to allow for more focused exploitation of good solutions.

- **Stagnation Detection:** If the algorithm detects that the population is stagnating (e.g., no significant improvement in fitness over several generations), it can temporarily increase the mutation rate to reintroduce diversity and explore new areas of the search space.

Algorithms with adaptive mutation and crossover rates are more resilient and flexible because they can adapt on the fly to the optimisation task at hand.

27.1. Evolutionary Computation and Machine Learning

Evolutionary Computation (EC) methods are inspired by nature and tackle optimisation problems stochastically. They can provide a trustworthy and effective solution to difficult challenges in real-world situations. Recently, EC techniques have been applied to increase both the performance and quality of Machine Learning (ML) models. Evolutionary approaches can be applied to all three stages of machine learning: pre-processing (e.g., feature selection and resampling), learning (e.g., parameter setting, membership functions, and neural network topology), and postprocessing (e.g., rule optimisation, decision tree/support vector pruning, and ensemble learning). This essay analyses the importance of EC algorithms in addressing various ML issues. We do not present a complete analysis of evolutionary ML approaches here; rather, we describe how EC algorithms can contribute to ML by tackling common difficulties in the artificial intelligence and ML areas. We examine the contributions of EC to machine learning in nine subfields: feature selection, resampling, classifiers, neural networks, reinforcement learning, clustering, association rule mining, and ensemble methods. For each category, we describe three components of evolutionary machine learning: issue formulation, search techniques, and fitness value computation.

The computational models using evolutionary algorithms apply evolutionary processes in order to solve complex problems. These evolutionary processes are inspired by biological evolution theory. Evolving algorithms use principles such as inheritance from previous successful generations, and natural selection where the best solutions pass their traits on to the successive generations.

Machine learning is a subfield of artificial intelligence, which is broadly defined as the capability of a machine to imitate intelligent human behavior. Artificial intelligence systems are used to perform complex tasks in a way that is similar to how humans solve problems.

The goal of AI is to create computer models that exhibit "intelligent behaviors" like humans, according to Boris katz, a principal research scientist and head of the InfoLab Group at CSAIL. This means machines that can recognize a visual scene, understand a text written in natural language, or perform an action in the physical world.

Machine learning is one way to use AI. It was defined in the 1950s by AI pioneer Arthur samuel as "the field of study that gives computers the ability to learn without explicitly being programmed."

Machine learning starts with data — numbers, photos, or text, like bank transactions, pictures of people or even bakery items, repair records, time series data from sensors, or sales reports. The data is gathered and prepared to be used as training data, or the information the machine learning model will be trained on. The more data, the better the program.

27.2. Evolutionary Computation and Optimization Techniques

Evolutionary computation is approximately 50 years old, beginning with John Holland's key work at the University of Michigan in 1975, which developed the genetic algorithm. Evolutionary computation refers to a set of problem-solving techniques that draw inspiration from natural evolutionary and genetic processes. The genetic algorithm is the most well-known form of evolutionary computation, which evolves a population of solutions to the problem at hand, each represented as a bit-string—the genotype—with a fitness function measuring the bit-string's fitness within the context of the problem (i.e., mapping a genotype to a phenotype). Evolutionary operators like as mutation, crossover, and selection govern the simulated evolution across multiple generations.

Evolutionary computation examples

Genetic algorithms are search heuristics that use the process of natural selection to find optimal solutions to optimisation and search issues. Genetic algorithms use crossover, mutation, and selection to evolve a population of solutions.

Genetic programming is a sort of evolutionary computation that creates computer programs to solve specified goals, which are often represented as trees. Genetic programming evolves the structure and behaviour of programs using operators related to genetic algorithms, such as crossover, mutation, and selection.

Evolutionary strategies are optimisation techniques that use self-adaptive mutation rates to explore the solution space. Evolutionary techniques often include a population of candidate solutions as well as a fitness-based selection process.

Tips for using evolutionary computation

Choose appropriate representations and operators for the problem at hand.

Use hybrid approaches that combine evolutionary computation with other optimization techniques for improved performance.

Consider parallel and distributed implementations to speed up the computation process.

Optimization Techniques

Machine learning methods and algorithms rely heavily on optimisation approaches to enhance their performance. Minimising or maximising an objective function—a loss function in supervised learning or some evaluation metric in unsupervised learning—is the main aim of optimisation in machine learning.

- **Gradient Descent**: a fundamental technique for decreasing loss functions by iterative model parameter updates that are made against the gradient. Momentum-based Gradient Descent, Mini-batch, and stochastic are some of the variations.

- **Adam Optimisation:** An adaptive learning rate method that adjusts based on running averages of gradients and their squared values. It often converges faster than standard gradient descent and requires less fine-tuning.

- **Hyperparameter Tuning:** the process of improving model performance by optimising hyperparameters utilising techniques like Grid Search, Random Search, and Bayesian Optimisation.

- **Regularization**: Techniques like L1, L2, Dropout, and Early Stopping help prevent overfitting by penalizing complexity and ensuring better generalization to unseen data.

28. *Integration with Other AI Techniques*

Integrating hybrid algorithms with other AI techniques involves combining the strengths of various AI methods—such as machine learning, fuzzy logic, expert systems, or neural networks—with optimization techniques like evolutionary algorithms, metaheuristics, and exact algorithms. This integration can enhance the performance of the AI system by providing more sophisticated decision-making, better adaptability, and improved optimization(V. Kumar & Yadav, 2022).

Below are common ways hybrid algorithms integrate with other AI techniques:

1. **Machine Learning and Metaheuristics:**

    Machine learning techniques (e.g., neural networks, support vector machines, decision trees) can be combined with metaheuristics (e.g., Genetic Algorithms, Particle Swarm

Optimization) to optimize model parameters, enhance learning, or handle complex search spaces.

- **Optimization of Hyperparameters:** Metaheuristics like Genetic Algorithms (GA) or Differential Evolution (DE) can be used to optimize hyperparameters of machine learning models. For example, using a GA to tune the hyperparameters of a neural network (e.g., learning rate, number of layers, and neurons).

- **Feature Selection:** Hybrid approaches can combine evolutionary algorithms with machine learning to automatically select relevant features from large datasets. For example, combining GA with a decision tree algorithm to select the most significant features.

Example:

- **Neuroevolution:** A combination of neural networks and evolutionary algorithms where the neural network architecture (topology) and/or weights are evolved using genetic algorithms. This method is particularly useful in reinforcement learning environments where traditional gradient-based methods may struggle.

- **Genetic Programming (GP):** A process whereby computer programs are trained to find solutions to specific problems. GP is often integrated with machine learning models to evolve decision rules or model structures for predictive tasks.

2. **Fuzzy Logic and Metaheuristics:**

- Fuzzy logic systems handle uncertainty and imprecision by using fuzzy sets and rules. When combined with metaheuristics, fuzzy logic can enhance decision-making, control systems, and optimization under uncertainty (Dubetcky, 2024).

- **Fuzzy Inference Systems:** Metaheuristic algorithms like Genetic Algorithms (GA), Particle Swarm Optimization (PSO), or Ant Colony Optimization (ACO) can optimize the membership functions and fuzzy rules in fuzzy inference systems (FIS). This integration improves the accuracy and adaptability of fuzzy systems in control applications and decision-making tasks.

Example:

- **Fuzzy-GA Systems:** These systems use a GA to optimize fuzzy membership functions and rule sets in fuzzy logic controllers, improving their adaptability in complex, dynamic environments such as robotics or industrial control.

- **Fuzzy-PSO:** In this hybrid, PSO is used to fine-tune fuzzy system parameters to optimize performance in tasks such as forecasting, decision support, or control systems.

3. **Expert Systems and Optimization:**

Expert systems use rule-based reasoning to emulate the decision-making ability of human experts. When combined with optimization algorithms, the hybrid system can enhance the reasoning process and solve more complex problems.

- **Rule Optimization:** Metaheuristics like Genetic Algorithms (GA) can optimize the rule base of expert systems by selecting or tuning rules that lead to better outcomes.

- **Knowledge Discovery:** Hybrid approaches can integrate machine learning with expert systems to automatically extract rules from data and refine the knowledge base of the expert system.

Example:

- **GA-Expert System:** In medical diagnosis, a genetic algorithm can be used to optimize the rules in an expert system, enhancing the system's diagnostic accuracy by identifying the most effective rule combinations.

- **Neuro-Fuzzy-Expert System:** Combining neural networks with fuzzy logic and expert systems, this hybrid system can learn from data (neural networks), handle uncertainty (fuzzy logic), and provide explainable decisions (expert systems).

4. **Neural Networks and Evolutionary Algorithms:**

Neural networks are powerful for pattern recognition, function approximation, and learning tasks. Evolutionary algorithms can optimize the structure, weights, or learning strategies of neural networks.

- **Neuroevolution:** Evolutionary algorithms can be used to evolve both the architecture and weights of neural networks. This is particularly useful in tasks where traditional backpropagation struggles, such as reinforcement learning or tasks with sparse rewards.

- **Hybrid Training:** Neural networks can be trained using metaheuristics like Genetic Algorithms (GA) or Particle Swarm Optimization (PSO) to escape local minima, especially in complex optimization landscapes.

Example:

- **NEAT (Neuroevolutionary of Augmenting Topologies):** An approach that evolves neural network architectures along with weights using evolutionary strategies. NEAT is effective in evolving complex neural network architectures for reinforcement learning problems.

- **PSO-NN:** A hybrid where PSO optimizes the weights of a neural network, leading to better convergence in some scenarios than traditional gradient-based methods, especially in cases with noisy data.

5. **Reinforcement Learning and Evolutionary Computation:**

Reinforcement learning (RL) is a framework where agents learn to make decisions by interacting with an environment. Evolutionary computation methods can be integrated with RL to improve exploration, handle sparse rewards, and optimize policies(Prathima, 2021).

- **Policy Optimization:** Evolutionary strategies (ES) can optimize the policy in reinforcement learning by searching for better parameter settings. This can complement traditional policy gradient methods, especially in environments with high-dimensional action spaces.

- **Exploration Strategies:** Evolutionary algorithms can be used to evolve exploration strategies in RL, helping the agent explore the environment more effectively when reward signals are sparse or deceptive.

Example:

- **Evolution Strategies in RL:** Evolutionary strategies (ES) can optimize policies in reinforcement learning by evolving a population of policies rather than relying on gradient-based methods. This approach can scale well in distributed settings.

- **Hybrid RL with GA:** Combining genetic algorithms with reinforcement learning allows the GA to explore different strategies and then use RL to refine them, making it suitable for complex environments with long decision horizons.

The integration of hybrid algorithms with other AI techniques provides a powerful way to tackle complex and diverse problems by leveraging the strengths of different methods. These integrated approaches can improve performance, adaptability, and robustness in optimization, learning, decision-making, and prediction tasks across various domains. However, designing and implementing such hybrids requires careful consideration to ensure that the different techniques complement each other effectively(Kamboj, 2024).

Neuroevolution: Evolutionary algorithms can be used to evolve both the architecture and weights of neural networks. This is particularly useful in tasks where traditional backpropagation struggles, such as reinforcement learning or tasks with sparse rewards.

28.1. Evolutionary Neural Networks

Evolutionary Neural Networks (EvoNN) represent a class of hybrid algorithms that combine the principles of evolutionary algorithms with neural networks. The goal is to optimize various aspects of neural networks—such as architecture, weights, hyperparameters, and training strategies—using evolutionary algorithms. This approach can help overcome some of the limitations of traditional neural network training methods, such as getting stuck in local minima, slow convergence, or the challenge of designing optimal network architectures.

Key Concepts in Evolutionary Neural Networks

1. **Neuroevolution:**

   - **Definition:** Neuroevolution refers to the application of evolutionary algorithms to optimize neural networks. This can involve evolving the network's architecture, connection weights, learning rules, or even the activation functions.

   - **Evolutionary Algorithms:** Algorithms like Genetic Algorithms (GA), Differential Evolution (DE), Particle Swarm Optimization (PSO), and Evolution Strategies (ES) are commonly used to evolve neural networks. These algorithms use a population of candidate solutions (neural networks) and apply evolutionary operations (e.g., selection, crossover, mutation) to optimize them over generations.

2. **Direct Encoding vs. Indirect Encoding:**

   - **Direct Encoding:** In direct encoding, each neural network is represented explicitly in the chromosome or genotype. This means that every weight, connection, and parameter is encoded in the individual's genome. Direct encoding is simpler but can become impractical for large networks due to the massive size of the search space(Kassahun et al., 2007).

   - **Indirect Encoding:** Indirect encoding represents neural networks in a more abstract way, such as using rules or patterns to generate the network. This allows for the evolution of more complex structures with fewer parameters, leading to potentially more efficient searches in the solution space.

3. **Fitness Function:**

- **Purpose:** The fitness function evaluates the performance of a neural network in solving a particular task (e.g., classification accuracy, error rate, or reward in reinforcement learning). The fitness function guides the selection of better-performing networks for reproduction in the next generation.

- **Multi-Objective Optimization:** In some cases, multiple objectives (e.g., accuracy and model complexity) are considered in the fitness function to evolve networks that balance performance with resource efficiency.

4. **Evolving Different Aspects of Neural Networks:**

- **Weight Evolution:** Evolutionary algorithms can optimize the weights of the neural network, potentially finding better solutions than traditional gradient-based methods like backpropagation, especially in noisy or non-differentiable environments.

- **Architecture Evolution:** Neural architecture search (NAS) can be performed using evolutionary algorithms to discover optimal network structures, such as the number of layers, neurons per layer, and connectivity patterns.

- **Activation Function Evolution:** In some cases, the activation functions themselves are evolved to find novel and effective non-linear transformations for neuron outputs.

- **Hyperparameter Evolution:** Parameters such as learning rate, batch size, and regularization terms can also be evolved, allowing the network to adapt its learning process more effectively.

Key Methods and Approaches

1. **Neuro Evolution of Augmenting Topologies (NEAT):**

- **Overview:** NEAT is a popular neuroevolution algorithm that evolves both the topology and weights of neural networks. It starts with simple networks and gradually adds complexity (e.g., adding nodes and connections) over generations, making it well-suited for reinforcement learning tasks and tasks with sparse rewards(Tatiwar, 2023).

- **Speciation:** NEAT uses speciation to protect innovative structures during evolution by grouping similar networks into species. This prevents premature convergence and allows new structures to evolve without being immediately outcompeted by established solutions.

2. **HyperNEAT:**

- **Extension of NEAT:** HyperNEAT extends NEAT by evolving Compositional Pattern-Producing Networks (CPPNs), which indirectly encode the neural network architecture. This allows for the generation of large-scale neural networks with regular patterns, making it suitable for tasks that require spatial or geometric relationships, such as image processing.

- **Indirect Encoding:** Instead of evolving each weight directly, HyperNEAT evolves a function that determines the connectivity of the neural network. This allows for the creation of complex networks with fewer parameters and facilitates the evolution of networks with regular and modular structures.

3. **Co-Evolutionary Methods:**

- **Co-Evolution:** In co-evolution, multiple populations of neural networks evolve simultaneously, where each population may represent a different aspect of the network (e.g., weights and topology). These populations interact and co-adapt, leading to more sophisticated solutions.

- **Competitive and Cooperative Co-Evolution:** In competitive co-evolution, networks evolve in an adversarial setting (e.g., evolving both an agent and its opponent in a game). In cooperative co-evolution, different parts of the solution evolve together to optimize a shared fitness function.

4. **Evolution Strategies (ES):**

- **Overview:** Evolution Strategies (ES) are optimization techniques that use a population of solutions and apply mutations and recombination to evolve them. In the context of neural networks, ES can optimize network weights by treating them as continuous parameters and evolving them over generations.

- **Gradient-Free Optimization:** Unlike backpropagation, ES does not rely on gradients, making it effective in environments where gradient information is unavailable or unreliable, such as in reinforcement learning with sparse rewards(Sakhuja, 2024).

5. **Differential Evolution (DE) for Neural Networks:**

- **Overview:** DE is an evolutionary algorithm that optimizes continuous parameters, such as the weights of a neural network. DE uses vector differences to guide mutations, making it a powerful method for fine-tuning network weights, especially in cases with complex error surfaces(Sakhuja, 2024).

- **Application:** DE can be particularly effective in optimizing neural networks for regression tasks, time-series forecasting, and other problems where gradient-based methods may struggle.

Applications of Evolutionary Neural Networks

1. **Reinforcement Learning:**

- **Neuroevolution:** Evolutionary algorithms are widely used in reinforcement learning (RL) to optimize policies (e.g., in deep RL), particularly when reward signals are sparse or delayed. Evolving neural networks can help RL agents discover effective strategies without the need for traditional gradient-based training.

- **Example:** In tasks like game playing (e.g., evolving controllers for video games), neuroevolution can discover policies that outperform those trained using traditional RL methods.

2. **Automated Neural Architecture Search (NAS):**

- **Architecture Evolution:** A procedure called neural architecture search (NAS) uses evolutionary algorithms to automate the search for ideal neural network topologies. This can lead to the discovery of novel architectures that outperform manually designed networks.

- **Example:** Google's AutoML and other NAS frameworks have successfully used evolutionary algorithms to discover state-of-the-art architectures for tasks like image classification and natural language processing.

3. **Optimization in Complex Environments:**

- **Weight Optimization:** Evolutionary algorithms can optimize neural network weights in complex environments where traditional gradient-based optimization methods, like backpropagation, may fail due to non-differentiable objectives or noisy data.

- **Example:** Evolving neural networks for robotic control in physical environments where sensor noise, delays, and uncertainties can make gradient-based learning challenging.

4. **Games and Simulations:**

- **Game AI:** Evolutionary neural networks are used to evolve game-playing agents that can learn strategies and tactics for competitive environments. Neuroevolution has been used in games like chess, Go, and real-time strategy games(MSc, 2024).

- **Simulation-Based Learning:** EvoNN can be applied in simulation environments to evolve neural controllers for autonomous vehicles, drones, and robots, allowing them to adapt to dynamic and unpredictable environments.

Advantages of Evolutionary Neural Networks

- **Gradient-Free Optimization:** EvoNN is well-suited for situations where traditional gradient-based approaches fail, such as those with non-differentiable or noisy fitness landscapes, because it does not depend on gradient information.

- **Exploration of Complex Architectures:** Evolutionary algorithms can explore novel and complex network architectures that may not be easily discovered through manual design or traditional methods.

Challenges of Evolutionary Neural Networks

- **Computational Cost:** Using evolutionary methods, particularly with deep neural networks, can be computationally expensive due to the huge number of candidate networks that are typically evaluated.

- **Scaling:** Finding efficient, optimal solutions is increasingly difficult as neural network sizes grow because the search space grows greater(D'souza et al., 2020).

- **Design of Fitness Functions:** A well-designed fitness function that accounts for the goals of the task and does not introduce any biases is crucial to EvoNN's performance.

Evolutionary Neural Networks (EvoNN) provide a powerful approach to optimizing neural networks by combining the exploratory capabilities of evolutionary algorithms with the learning capacity of neural networks. This hybrid approach can overcome some limitations of traditional training methods, making it applicable to a wide range of tasks, including reinforcement learning, neural architecture search, and optimization in complex environments. Despite challenges like computational cost, EvoNN continues to be a valuable tool in the field of artificial intelligence, particularly in scenarios where traditional methods fall short.

28.2. Hybrid Systems with Fuzzy Logic

Complex, uncertain, and imprecise issues can be effectively solved by hybrid systems that combine fuzzy logic with other computational techniques. A number of artificial intelligence techniques, including expert systems, neural networks, and evolutionary algorithms, can benefit from fuzzy logic's capacity to deal with ambiguity and approximate thinking. These hybrid systems use the best features of both methods to provide smarter, more resilient systems(Melin & Castillo, 2005).

Overview of Fuzzy Logic

Fuzzy logic is a form of multi-valued logic that allows for reasoning about imprecision and uncertainty. Instead of binary true/false outcomes, fuzzy logic deals with degrees of truth, representing values between 0 and 1. This makes it well-suited for problems involving vague or imprecise information, such as decision-making under uncertainty, control systems, and pattern recognition.

In hybrid systems, fuzzy logic is often used to enhance adaptability, handle uncertainty, or model human-like reasoning, while other techniques may optimize, learn, or provide structure to the system.

Types of Hybrid Systems with Fuzzy Logic

1. **Neuro-Fuzzy Systems:**

   - **Overview:** By fusing neural networks' learning capabilities with fuzzy logic's interpretability and reasoning, neuro-fuzzy systems are created. Building systems with neural network-like data learning capabilities and fuzzy logic-like reasoning and decision-making capabilities is the target.

   - **How it Works:** Fuzzy logic is responsible for thinking and decision-making, while neural networks are used to learn membership functions and fuzzy rules from data. The resulting system can learn from experience and generalize well to new data, making it suitable for tasks like classification, prediction, and control.

   Examples:

   - **Adaptive Neuro-Fuzzy Inference System (ANFIS):** ANFIS integrates neural networks with fuzzy inference systems, allowing the system to automatically adjust the membership functions and rules based on input-output data. This makes ANFIS effective for tasks such as time-series forecasting and adaptive control.

- **Neuro-Fuzzy Control:** In robotics and industrial automation, neuro-fuzzy control systems learn from experience to handle complex and dynamic environments, where traditional control methods may fail (M. Kumar & Garg, 2005).

2. **Genetic Fuzzy Systems (GFS):**

- **Overview:** Genetic fuzzy systems optimise fuzzy inference system structure, membership functions, or fuzzy rules by combining fuzzy logic with evolutionary algorithms, most often Genetic Algorithms. In order to improve the system's efficiency and accuracy, the evolutionary algorithm seeks for the optimal set of fuzzy rules or parameters.

- **How it Works:** A genetic algorithm uses chromosomes to encode possible solutions, such as membership functions or fuzzy rules. The fuzzy system is optimised as these chromosomes evolve through generations of selection, mutation, and crossover. By measuring how well the fuzzy system completes a given task, the fitness function determines its overall quality.

<u>Examples:</u>

- **GA-Tuned Fuzzy Controllers:** Genetic algorithms can be used to tune the parameters of a fuzzy logic controller in real-time, optimizing performance for applications such as autonomous driving, process control, or robot navigation.

- **Fuzzy Rule Optimization:** In classification or decision-making systems, a genetic algorithm can evolve a set of fuzzy rules to maximize classification accuracy or decision quality.

3. **Fuzzy Expert Systems:**

- **Overview:** Fuzzy expert systems extend traditional rule-based expert systems by incorporating fuzzy logic to handle uncertainty and imprecision. This makes the system more flexible and capable of dealing with vague or incomplete information.

- **How it Works:** Fuzzy expert systems use fuzzy rules (if-then rules with fuzzy sets) instead of crisp logic rules. These systems can reason with imprecise inputs and produce outputs that are not just binary decisions but include degrees of certainty.

<u>Examples:</u>

- **Medical Diagnosis Systems:** Fuzzy expert systems are often used in medical diagnosis to handle uncertainty in symptoms and test results. By using fuzzy logic, these systems can better mimic human reasoning, offering more nuanced diagnostic outcomes(Awotunde et al., 2014).

- **Financial Decision Support Systems:** Fuzzy logic can be used in financial expert systems to model uncertainty in market conditions, helping in investment decision-making or risk assessment.

4. **Fuzzy Logic with Particle Swarm Optimization (PSO):**

- **Overview:** The population-based optimisation method known as Particle Swarm Optimisation (PSO) takes its cues from the cooperative actions of fish and birds. When combined with fuzzy logic, PSO can optimize fuzzy systems, especially in tasks involving high-dimensional search spaces or multi-objective optimization.

- **How it Works:** Fuzzy systems often employ PSO to fine-tune their parameters, including membership functions and rule weights. The particles in PSO represent potential solutions, and they explore the solution space by following their own experience and that of their neighbors, leading to optimized fuzz

5. **Fuzzy Logic and Reinforcement Learning (RL):**

- **Overview:** Fuzzy logic can be combined with reinforcement learning to create adaptive systems that can learn optimal actions in uncertain or dynamic environments. Fuzzy rules handle decision-making, while reinforcement learning optimizes these rules based on feedback from the environment.

- **How it Works:** The system starts with a set of fuzzy rules that govern decision-making. As the system interacts with the environment, reinforcement learning algorithms adjust these fuzzy rules to improve performance over time. The combination allows for adaptive behavior in complex environments where both uncertainty and learning are essential.

<u>Examples:</u>

- **Fuzzy-RL Controllers:** In autonomous robotics, fuzzy-reinforcement learning controllers can learn to navigate dynamic environments by continuously adjusting their fuzzy rules based on environmental feedback.

- **Fuzzy-Q Learning:** In this approach, Q-learning (a popular RL algorithm) is combined with fuzzy logic to handle continuous state-action spaces. This is useful in tasks like robotic control or game AI, where the environment is complex and hard to model explicitly.

<u>Applications of Hybrid Fuzzy Systems</u>

- **Control Systems:** Hybrid fuzzy systems are widely used in control applications, such as temperature control, traffic management, or robotic control. The combination of fuzzy logic and other AI techniques allows for adaptive, real-time control in complex, uncertain environments (Tai et al., 2016).

- **Pattern Recognition and Classification:** Pattern recognition activities, such as image processing, speech recognition, and handwriting analysis, make use of hybrid systems that integrate fuzzy logic with neural networks or evolutionary algorithms. While the other methods improve classification accuracy, fuzzy logic aids in dealing with data imprecision and noise.

- **Optimization:**Fuzzy-augmented evolutionary algorithms are used for optimization tasks in engineering design, logistics, and resource allocation. The hybrid system can better handle multi-objective optimization problems with conflicting objectives and uncertain constraints.

- **Decision Support Systems:** In areas like finance, healthcare, and supply chain management, hybrid fuzzy systems provide decision support by modeling uncertainty, optimizing decision rules, and adapting to changing conditions.

- **Robotics and Autonomous Systems:** Hybrid systems combining fuzzy logic with reinforcement learning, neural networks, or evolutionary algorithms are used in robotics for tasks like navigation, object recognition, and interaction with dynamic environments. These systems enable robots to make adaptive, real-t

29. *Chapter Summary*

This chapter explored the growing field of adaptive and hybrid approaches in evolutionary computation and artificial intelligence. Algorithms may now self-tune parameters like mutation and crossover rates with the help of adaptive evolutionary computation, which improves their performance and makes searches more efficient. With adaptable mutation/crossover rates and self-adaptive parameters, evolutionary algorithms may alter their tactics on the fly to solve different problems, eliminating the need for human tuning.

Hybrid algorithms combine evolutionary computation with machine learning and optimization techniques, creating systems that can both learn from data and optimize complex search spaces. Evolutionary computation has been successfully integrated with various AI techniques, such as neural networks and fuzzy logic, resulting in powerful hybrid systems that can tackle a wide range of complex problems.

Evolutionary neural networks leverage the optimization capabilities of evolutionary algorithms to evolve neural network architectures and weights, making them particularly valuable in tasks like reinforcement learning and complex optimization. Hybrid systems with fuzzy logic use the reasoning capabilities of fuzzy logic to handle uncertainty, while evolutionary algorithms and neural networks provide optimization and learning capabilities.

Overall, the chapter highlighted the potential of adaptive and hybrid approaches to create more flexible, robust, and intelligent systems that can solve increasingly complex and dynamic problems in AI and beyond.

Part 1: (Very Short Questions)

1. What are self-adaptive parameters in evolutionary computation?

2. How do adaptive mutation rates benefit evolutionary algorithms?

3. What is the role of adaptive crossover rates in evolutionary computation?

4. How are evolutionary algorithms combined with machine learning techniques?

5. What are hybrid algorithms in the context of evolutionary computation?

6. How do evolutionary algorithms improve optimization techniques?

7. What are evolutionary neural networks?

8. How can fuzzy logic be integrated with evolutionary systems?

9. What advantages do hybrid AI systems offer?

10. How do self-adaptive parameters influence algorithm performance?

Part 2: (Short Questions)

1. What are self-adaptive parameters in adaptive evolutionary computation?

2. How do adaptive mutation and crossover rates improve evolutionary algorithms?

3. How can hybrid algorithms combine evolutionary computation with machine learning?

4. What are evolutionary neural networks, and how are they applied?

5. How does integrating fuzzy logic with evolutionary computation enhance hybrid systems?

Part 3: (Long Questions)

1. How do self-adaptive parameters in evolutionary computation improve the efficiency and robustness of optimization algorithms? Discuss the mechanisms through which self-adaptive strategies adjust mutation and crossover rates, and provide examples of how these adaptations can lead to better convergence rates and solution quality in complex optimization problems.

2. What are the theoretical foundations behind adaptive mutation and crossover rates in evolutionary algorithms, and how do these adaptive mechanisms influence the performance of evolutionary computation methods? Explore the impact of dynamically adjusting these rates based on the algorithm's current state and problem landscape, and discuss any trade-offs involved in these adaptations.

3. In what ways can hybrid algorithms that combine evolutionary computation with machine learning techniques offer advantages over traditional methods? Examine specific applications where such hybrids have been effective, and discuss how evolutionary algorithms can be used to enhance the training, feature selection, or hyperparameter optimization processes in machine learning models.

4. How do evolutionary computation techniques integrate with other optimization methods to form hybrid algorithms? Discuss the synergistic benefits of combining evolutionary algorithms with gradient-based methods, metaheuristic approaches, or other optimization techniques, and provide examples of real-world problems where such hybrid approaches have achieved superior results.

5. What are the benefits and challenges associated with integrating evolutionary neural networks with fuzzy logic systems? Analyze how evolutionary algorithms can be employed to optimize neural network architectures or fuzzy rule bases, and discuss the potential improvements in decision-making and adaptability that arise from such hybrid systems. Consider practical applications where this integration has been successfully implemented.

Part 4: (MCQs)

1. What does "self-adaptive parameters" in evolutionary computation refer to?

    a. Parameters that remain constant throughout the evolution process

    b. Parameters that are fixed manually by the user

    c. Parameters that adjust automatically during the evolution process

    d. Parameters that are only used for initialization

2. In evolutionary algorithms, what is the primary purpose of adaptive mutation rates?

    a. To reduce the number of generations needed for convergence

    b. To automatically adjust the rate of mutation based on the search process

    c. To ensure that all solutions are mutated equally

    d. To fix the mutation rate to avoid excessive changes

3. Why are adaptive crossover rates important in evolutionary computation?

    a. To maintain a fixed crossover probability for consistency

    b. To change the crossover rate dynamically based on the performance of the population

    c. To ensure that crossover occurs only once per generation

    d. To avoid the use of crossover in the algorithm

4. What is a primary benefit of combining evolutionary computation with machine learning?

   a. It simplifies the evolutionary algorithms

   b. It allows for automatic adjustment of parameters without learning

   c. It enhances optimization and learning capabilities by leveraging both approaches

   d. It eliminates the need for machine learning techniques

5. In the context of evolutionary computation, what is the role of optimization techniques?

   a. To improve the efficiency and effectiveness of evolutionary algorithms

   b. To replace evolutionary algorithms with more efficient methods

   c. To limit the search space to predefined bounds

   d. To only handle discrete optimization problems

6. What does the integration of evolutionary neural networks involve

   a. Using neural networks solely for feature extraction

   b. Combining neural networks with evolutionary algorithms to optimize their parameters

   c. Replacing evolutionary algorithms with neural networks

   d. Ensuring neural networks function independently of evolutionary algorithms

7. In hybrid systems that include fuzzy logic, what is the main advantage of combining it with evolutionary computation?

   a. To simplify the design of fuzzy rules

   b. To automatically generate fuzzy rules and membership functions through evolutionary processes

   c. To eliminate the need for fuzzy logic in the system

   d. To restrict the use of fuzzy logic to specific problems

8. Which of the following best describes a hybrid system in the context of AI?

    a. A system that uses only one AI technique for all tasks

    b. A system that integrates multiple AI techniques to leverage their combined strengths

    c. A system that eliminates the use of AI techniques

    d. A system that only focuses on theoretical AI concepts

9. What is the primary goal of integrating evolutionary computation with optimization techniques?

    a. To replace evolutionary computation with purely optimization techniques

    b. To enhance the ability to solve complex optimization problems by leveraging evolutionary strategies

    c. To simplify optimization problems to avoid the need for evolutionary algorithms

    d. To focus solely on the theoretical aspects of optimization

10. How can hybrid systems with fuzzy logic improve decision-making processes?

    a. By reducing the number of decisions made

    b. By providing a flexible and interpretable approach to handling uncertainty and imprecision in decision-making

    c. By removing the need for human input in decision-making

    d. By focusing only on binary decision-making scenarios

Answer

1	2	3	4	5	6	7	8	9	10
c	b	b	c	a	b	b	b	b	b

CHAPTER 6

APPLICATIONS IN NEXT-GEN AI

30. Introduction

In today's fast-paced digital environment, keeping up with user demands in an increasingly tech-savvy society is a huge issue for traditional library management systems. The NextGen Library is a game-changing solution that uses cutting-edge tech to transform library services and tackles these issues head-on. Designed to meet the needs of contemporary library patrons and staff, NextGen Library revolutionises library administration with its seamless integration of AI and Near Field Communication (NFC) technologies.

Libraries have always been places where people may go to find a wealth of information, acting as repository of knowledge. A paradigm change in library management procedures is required, however, due to the fact that digital technologies have changed the way users access and interact with information.

The NextGen Library has taken the initiative to implement AI-driven solutions in order to improve user experiences, optimise operations, and allocate resources more efficiently, all because they understand the need of adapting. Users are able to effortlessly peruse the library's extensive collection thanks to the platform's real-time response mechanisms and personalised recommendations, creating an experience that is both interesting and dynamic. Furthermore, libraries can now keep better tabs on their inventory with the use of

NFC technology, which allows for exact book identification and smooth transaction operations. The adoption of near field communication (NFC) devices allows users to quickly obtain book information, verify availability, and start the borrowing or return process, which improves operational efficiency and user happiness. Furthermore, NextGen Library promotes diversity and accessibility in library services with its user-centric design and intuitive interface, which cater to users of various technical proficiencies. When it comes to managing libraries, NextGen Library is a game-changer. It provides a one-stop shop for all of the problems that modern library patrons and staff face. Through the utilisation of AI and NFC technology, the platform revolutionises the library experience, enabling users to engage with knowledge in new and exciting ways through exploration, discovery, and inventive use of their data. In this research study, we examine NextGen Library in detail, dissecting its features, capabilities, and prospective influence on library services in the future.

31. Optimization Problems

Finding a function's minimum or maximum value is a typical use of calculus. For instance, maximising income and minimising production costs are common business objectives. Reducing the quantity of material needed to package a product of a given volume is frequently a goal in manufacturing. Here we demonstrate how to formulate and solve such minimisation and maximisation issues using the methods covered in this chapter.

Solving Optimization Problems over a Closed, Bounded Interval

The following optimisation challenges have the same basic premise. Whether we can maximise or minimise a certain quantity is of importance to us. But there are auxiliary conditions that must be met as well. Maximising the area of a rectangular garden is of relevance in Example 4.7.1, for instance. It stands to reason that the area will keep growing as long as we keep extending the garden's sides. But what if there's a limit to the amount of fencing we can deploy around the perimeter? Given these constraints, we will not be able to create a garden of our dreams. How can we find the optimal solution for maximising the area of a rectangle given a perimeter constraint?

The garden will be built in a rectangle shape with a rock wall along one side and three sides bordered by wire fencing (Figure 4.7.1). Calculate the optimal dimensions for a garden that would make the most efficient use of 100 feet of wire fencing. How big can it get?

31.1. Scheduling and Routing

Routing is at the core of what we do here at SmartRoutes. Our mission is to ensure that the routes that businesses use to deliver and serve their customers are the most efficient and optimal they can be. This is ultimately what drives huge cost savings and improves experiences for our customers.

However, route scheduling is something we also pay particular attention to in the development of our delivery management software.

While route planning, route optimization, and route scheduling are all inextricably linked in the delivery planning process, each one plays its own role in the success of a logistics operation.

In this blog, we'll take a look at what exactly route scheduling involves, why it is important, who it affects in a delivery business, and who is ultimately responsible for the task in a transport business

- What is Route Scheduling?

- Why is Route Scheduling Important?

- What is The Difference Between Route Scheduling and Route Planning?

- How Does SmartRoutes Optimize Routing and Scheduling?

What is Route Scheduling?

Route scheduling refers to the process of planning and optimizing routes by utilizing the available resources to their best effect. The key resources referred to include vehicles, drivers, driver mates, and depot and warehouse staff needed to assist with loading before the departure of vehicles.

Route scheduling can require transport managers and route planners to account for a host of factors the availability of drivers, defined working hours, driver regulations around breaks and rest periods, and customers' own delivery schedules.

When all this is considered, it can make the task of scheduling routes difficult given the large number of stakeholders with competing interests. For example, a driver may wish to make a delivery before 4:00 P.M in order to finish their working day on time, but a customer may wish to have their delivery after 5:00 P.M to avoid it affecting their regular business operations.

The demands placed upon transport and logistics managers in today's world mean that this is often an impossible task to complete manually, and route optimization software plays a key role in automating the best route schedules based on hundreds of parameters.

Why is Route Scheduling Important?

Getting route scheduling right is critically important to the overall success of a delivery service. Given the significant role that delivery plays in contemporary retail, a well-performing delivery service is often mission-critical for the success of the wider business.

From a commercial perspective, a robust scheduling process ensures that businesses are maximizing two of their most critical resources; their drivers and their fleet.

Ensuring that schedules are created in an efficient and predictable manner helps businesses cut costs and provide an optimal delivery experience to customers.

However, what is often overlooked when considering the importance of route scheduling, is the driver's level of satisfaction. Drivers, like us all, have lives outside of their 9-5. Having a schedule that meets their personal needs and that provides them with a level of predictability can be the difference whether you have a happy, productive workforce or otherwise. In fact, in a survey conducted by Route Smart, amongst 28 leading delivery company executives surveyed, 90% of respondents agreed that there is a direct correlation between driver satisfaction and customer satisfaction.

31.2. Parameter Tuning and Configuration

The values of several choices, known as hyperparameters, control the training process and determine the quality of the predictive model created by PROC GRADBOOST. Not all applications might benefit from these hyperparameters' default values. The AUTOTUNE statement can find the optimal values for these hyperparameters, saving you time and effort when tweaking them by hand. By utilising the AUTOTUNE statement, the optimisation algorithm (tuner) endeavours to minimise the objective function by exploring potential combinations of values for these selected hyperparameters. For nominal goals, the objective function is the estimate of the validation error, which is the misclassification error. For interval targets, it is the average square error. Iterations are a part of tuning, and with each iteration comes the evaluation of several goal functions. Each objective function evaluation can consist of one or several training and scoring executions as follows:

- The tuner employs a single-partition validation set as specified in the PARTITION statement. A new model is trained on the training subset for each freshly created configuration of hyperparameters. Then, the trained model is used to score the validation subset, yielding the value of the objective function.

- A single-partition validation set is used by the tuner when the FRACTION= option is specified. At this stage, the tuner divides the total data set into two portions: one for training the model and the other for validating it. A new model is trained on the training subset for each freshly created configuration of hyperparameters. Then, the trained model is used to score the validation subset, yielding the value of the objective function.

- The tuner employs k-fold cross validation when KFOLD=k is given. As part of this procedure, the tuner divides the data into k-fold portions, or folds. Each fold undergoes validation using the chosen (holdout) fold after a new model is trained on all (k-1) of the folds. A single error estimate value is obtained by averaging the objective function value over each set of training and scoring executions.

Genetic algorithms (GAs) provide the foundation for optimisation tuner algorithms; these GAs use evolution and natural selection to discover optimal configurations. Here is the order of operations that the tuner follows:

1. The first evaluation, called Iteration 0, uses a default model configuration, which is the default values of some model tuning parameters. One can use k-fold cross validation or single partition validation to get the objective function value, and then they record it for comparison.

2. The first group of configurations, or "population," is created by use of a method known as random Latin hypercube sampling (LHS). 1. For the purpose of comparison, the objective function values of each hyperparameter configuration are recorded and assessed in a Latin hypercube sample. Now we enter Iteration 1.

3. Iteration 2 is comprised of the best model configurations from the initial population, and they are evaluated along with the following population of configurations. So long as either the maximum time or the maximum number of evaluations are not achieved, this process is repeated for the remaining iterations.

4. A single training and model scoring run is used to review the optimal model configuration, and data regarding this configuration's training and score is returned.

5. As mentioned in the section on ODS Table Names, all model configurations that are evaluated are ranked. The values of the hyperparameters and objective functions for the top 10 configurations are returned in the Tuner Results ODS table.

You can tune the following hyperparameter values when you specify the AUTOTUNE statement:

- the LASSO= option for the L1 regularization parameter

- the RIDGE= option for the L2 regularization parameter

- the LEARNINGRATE= option for the learning rate parameter

- the NTREES= option for the number of trees

- the SAMPLINGRATE= option for the proportion of the training data to sample

- the VARS_TO_TRY= option for the number of variables to randomly select at each node split for each tree.

32. *Robotics and Automation*

Research in robotics focusses on developing and studying devices that can autonomously or semi-automatically carry out tasks defined by algorithms and programs that are both static and dynamic. These machines, sometimes known as robots, can be operated by humans or by a combination of human input and computer algorithms. Building, designing, and programming robots are all part of robotics, which is a broad subject. These machines have direct interaction with the physical environment and have frequently replaced humans in mundane and repetitive jobs. Later on, we'll talk about how robots can be classified according to their size, application domain, or purpose.

Robotics vs automation

Robotics is just one subset of automation. What this means is that processes can be executed entirely or in part without the need for human involvement. Computer programs, either static or dynamically updated, and mechanical or electrical machinery are the only operators of the process. Algorithms with all their actions predefined and executed separately, ignoring environmental changes, are what we mean when we talk about preconfigured applications.

When an algorithm is capable of adaptive automation, it can modify its actions in response to changes in the surrounding process or environment.

In most cases, robots are integrated into automated systems, which is why robotics and automation go hand in hand. While automation and robotics go hand in hand, there are situations in which robots are employed in conjunction with little to no automation. On the other hand, automation can exist independently of robotics.

The types of robots

Robots can be classified in different ways. We'll look at four main methods of categorisation:

- Size

- Application domain

- Purpose

- Number

Nanorobots or nanobots: To put that in perspective, a human red blood cell is approximately 5-10 micrometres in size, therefore you can see that nanorobots are built of nanomaterials and can range in size from 0.1 to 10 micrometres. While the idea of nanobots is currently being considered for potential medical applications, much more research and development time is required before they can be considered as a viable answer. A potential use for nanorobots is the diagnosis and treatment of disease through intravenous injection.

Microbots, millibots and minibots: These tiny robots, which are bigger than nanobots but yet not very big, do in fact exist. Smaller than 1 mm, 1 cm, and 10 cm, respectively, are microbots, millibots, and minibots. The tiniest flying robot, RoboBee, weighs 80 milligrammes and has a wingspan of 1.2 cm. The robot can be operated remotely and its wings can flap 120 times per second. The purpose of this little device is to create a flying swarm for purposes such as artificial pollination or search and rescue missions.

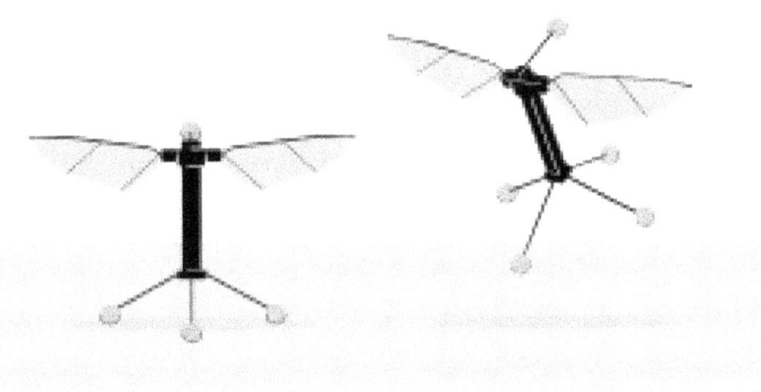

Source: - (Diem Redux, 2015)

Small and mid-sized robots: The usual dimensions of these robots range from 100 cm (small) to 100–200 cm (mid-sized), which is roughly the same as a human body. The majority of robots, toys, social robots, humanoids (robots that resemble people; think the popular comic book and movie characters Transformers), and computerised personal assistants are about this size. Most of the robots we encounter, both in fiction and in real life, are of the small to medium size.

Large robots: We are dwarfed by these mechanical beings. Significantly larger. Huge, eight to ten-metre-tall, humanoid robots do exist. Big, humanoid robots, on the other hand, are usually more for show than anything else. Large robots designed for use in factory automation, building sites, farms, autonomous vehicles, and navigation systems sometimes don't resemble humans at all.

Application domain

Robots can also be classified into personal and industrial robots based on their application domain..

- **Personal robots** are always there for us, and they're made to be practical for both individuals and families. Personal robots can be operated by individuals without technical expertise to carry out mundane and repetitive chores, either to save time or to provide entertainment. The most prevalent types of personal robots include social robots, digital assistants, toys, and robots used around the house.

- **Industrial robots** are sturdy and designed to carry out predetermined tasks in industries such as agriculture, construction, and manufacturing. Among its many uses are mounting, assembly, disassembly, welding, painting, visual inspection, and tightening screws. One thing that industrial robots excel at is being dependable, accurate, and quick machines. Modern technological advancement would be impossible without industrial robots.

Purpose: Robots can also be categorised according to their purpose. There are two types of robot purposes: particular and generic. But how is that meaningful?

- **Task-specific robots:** These devices carry out a certain task or a set of related duties. A social robot with a sophisticated natural language interface is on one extreme, and a robot arm that transports objects from point A to point B on the other. Because they are programmed to perform a certain task, these robots cannot be altered in any way, shape, or form. Some examples of such machines are industrial robots and household robots.

- **General-purpose robots:** In this scenario, the robot's job is up in the air. The robots' many parts can be purchased individually, and then put together in various ways to accomplish different duties. Robot arms, wheels, cameras, step motors, and other sensors and actuators could be part of the components. Some of these robots may even be able to connect wirelessly using Bluetooth and Wi-Fi. A small computer, the "brain" of the robot, can be "trained" to use various parts to carry out specific tasks by means of specialised applications developed using computer programming languages. Raspberry Pi, Arduino, Nvidia Jetson, and Jetson Nano are common examples of embedded systems, which are small computers that can be programmed. A common communication interface allows sensors and actuators to be linked to these embedded systems through their general-purpose input and output connections (GPIOs).

A prefabricated body with sensors (such as microphones and cameras) and actuators (such as limbs and arms) is another feature of general-purpose robots. It is possible to program the robot to carry out a wide variety of activities by modifying its software. The Nao, Pepper, and Romeo robots from Softbank Robotics are a few examples, as is Spot, the robot "dog" from Boston Dynamics.

- **Single robots:** autonomously completes tasks. In accordance with an established protocol, it carries out a certain task. Even if the robot is linked to the internet and has sophisticated programming that allows it to adapt to its surroundings, it is still just a robot. Since they are unable to exchange information with one another, even a cluster of singular robots is still considered to be "alone."

- **Robots in teams:** Similar to humans, robots are capable of working in teams. Multiple robots will often work in tandem to complete a job. Consider video documentation of the assembly process for automobiles. After the chassis is welded, the doors are added, the car is painted, the windows, both front and back, and the process continues thereafter. Separate robots specialised in each of these processes carry them out.

- **Swarm robotics:** Swarming is another way robots can operate. Here, a plethora of basic robots are guided by a single operator. While no one swarm robot is worth much on its own, the collective intelligence of the swarm may accomplish remarkable things. Consider bees in their natural habitat. Even if a single bee can't accomplish much, it's safe to say that humans couldn't have evolved without swarms of bees. Exploration, rescue, microbiology, monitoring, and pollination are some of the potential uses of swarm robotics. That being said, swarm robots is still very much in its early stages of development (2021).

The evolution of robots

The Czech term "robota" is the origin of the English word "robot"; it means "serf work" in English. The word "robot" became famous from Karel Čapek's 1920 play, in which machines rule the world. However, questioning the meaning of life has always piqued the curiosity of the human race. A number of stories describing those who succeeded in creating a human likeness existed even before the twentieth century. Paracelsus, an alchemist from the 16th century, is credited with one of the most well-known theories. He claimed that a tiny, humanoid creature (a homunculus) could be made in a petri dish by employing purely chemical processes. People started talking about golems later in the 1600s. The clay golem would serve its master if a person placed a parchment into its mouth or forehead, according to a folktale. According to the narrative, the golem eventually betrayed its maker after facing him head-on.

When we examine the evolution of robotics, we see a consistent desire to give robots personality and intelligence. There are typically three primary requirements for this interest:

- the robot has to be similar to a human being in some way (in appearance, in thinking, etc.)

- the robot has to be better at something (stronger, smarter, etc.)

- the robot has to be completely under the control of its creator

A watershed moment in robotics occurred with the advent of superhumanly powerful machines. During the first industrial revolution, which began in the 1760s, machines that could do the job of humans became increasingly common. Increasing the quantity of products while decreasing the amount of time and money spent on production was the primary goal back then. At that time, automation was the dominant idea. Automation allows for the completion of several procedures with little or no human involvement. People had to come up with new methods of living and working as machines started doing their jobs. Machines are able to work nonstop because they do not experience fatigue. With automation, both the quantity of waste and the danger of error were reduced. Controlled precision and efficacy are other traits of robots. There was no such thing as a computer in the 1800s. But humans also managed to build massive machines that could carry out complicated jobs. Significant progress in robots has been made since 1950.

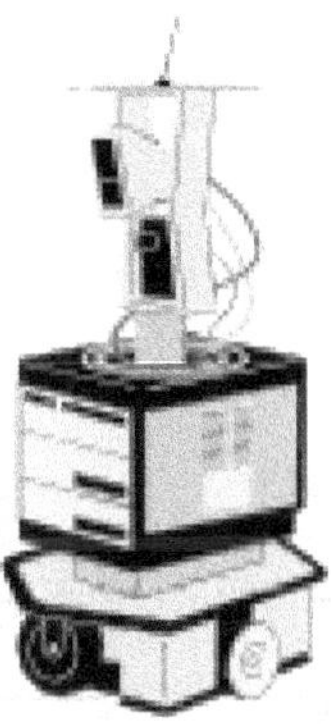

Source: - (Diem Redux, 2015)

There are many good things that can be said about robots, but people still aren't happy about them. People eager to work put constant pressure on the job market, which is problematic because technology may easily replace humans in routine jobs. Anxieties about robots taking over human jobs or being too controlling is a common concern when discussing robotics.

One more thing to be afraid of when robots get more lifelike. Most people can get along with robots that look like them. Humanoid robots that resemble robots can be easily classified by our brains in the same way as industrial robots are classified. When encountering a robot that is too lifelike, humans may feel bewildered and even irritated. As far as we can tell, this is a robot. But because it seems so genuine, the brain just can't process it. Its skin, motion, and speech are remarkably humanlike, but our brain has a hard time classifying it as a robot. Could it be thinking? Am I able to put my faith in it?

32.1. Evolutionary Robotics

Could we begin the robotic evolution if we can create sufficiently intelligent and capable robots? This would mean that robots would be able to build themselves.

Source: - (Healthcare Robot, 2024)

Although the concept of evolutionary robotics is not new, it does have the ring of science fiction. In the 1950s, Alan Turing argued that human designers would have a hard time creating intelligent robots and that a method that incorporates "mutations" and selective reproduction could be better. In actuality, the tools needed to implement evolutionary robotics have just recently been available, even though the idea itself is much older.

Everything needed to support evolutionary robotics is now at our fingertips, thanks to recent developments such as 3D printing, which allows for rapid prototyping and physical reproduction, neural networks, which aid in learning and training, longer battery life, cheaper materials, and much more. It is impossible for humans to write the evolutionary coding that would allow a robot to evolve. The term "evolution by design" describes a method of natural selection that is both random and disorderly. Thus, a complete shift in perspective is required if we are to realise the dream of evolutionary robots.

The term "evolutionary robotics" is a bit misleading since it actually means applying the same principles of evolution to systems that are not biological. Perhaps "embodied evolution" or "artificial evolution" would be more appropriate terms to use. The procedures themselves are evolving, rather than the robots themselves.

If a neural network and evolutionary algorithms could be programmed into any organism, it would be possible to create "offspring" from several parents by combining the genetic material of each and then recombinating the DNA. Actually, evolution doesn't even need a physical form; in fact, the same mechanisms may be employed to address critical problems in supercomputers.

To create robots that can interact intelligently and independently in the real world, evolutionary robotics is the only way to go. Robotic firefighters, search-and-rescue teams, robots to clean up nuclear waste, robots to assist with household chores, and many other potential uses for such robots are just a few examples of the numerous potential benefits.

Organic evolution could potentially be better understood. It's hard to fathom how a deeper comprehension of evolution might have such wide-ranging consequences. With any luck, we'll learn how to live longer, live healthier lives, lessen our impact on the environment, and figure out what the future holds for our species.

While the concept of iterative design—which involves making small adjustments to an existing design through repeated replication—is not new, its use in the real world has been limited to computer simulations up until now. It is possible to recreate an evolutionary process similar to natural selection in real biology by creating a virtual collection of replicable organisms. The more prosperous species tend to reproduce more frequently and with a more distinctive pattern. As a result, after a few generations, you will have a highly improved version of the organism that no human designer could have imagined.

Evolution through natural selection There are several benefits of using computer simulations. Theoretically, the only limit on the number of generations and their creation rate is the speed of the computer. Potentially useful ideas can be rapidly evaluated, while models with little promise can be easily rejected. Computer memory is abundant, cheap, and takes up very little space, so there's no need for a big supply of raw materials.

The problem is that it's possible the virtual organisms won't look anything like the real thing. In contrast, most physically producible robots have remained in the same form factor during their whole lives. The plan is to merge the two methods so that robots can plan and construct their own offspring, who will in turn plan and construct their own offspring, and so on.

The end outcome will be far beyond our wildest dreams (and that is the point). Robots might spend their days and nights brainstorming, constructing, and iterating on new robot types before putting them through test courses to find out what qualities the next generation should have. Robots do all the work.

32.2. Adaptive Control Systems

A popular type of control system, adaptive control systems (ACS) can change their actions and output depending on data sent by the system they're controlling. In essence, these systems adapt to their operating environments by learning from them and adjusting their parameters to maximise performance while reducing the effect of uncertainties or changes in system dynamics.

<u>**Key Characteristics of Adaptive Control Systems**</u>:

- **Dynamic Adaptability**: An adaptive control system's main trait is its ability to modify its behaviour. It does this by adjusting its parameters and control rules in response to changes occurring either within the system being controlled or in the external environment.

- **Real-time Tuning:** By constantly optimising performance and minimising errors, adaptive control systems differ from traditional control systems in that they fine-tune their operation based on real-time feedback.

- **Proactive Control:** The proactive nature of ACS stems from its capacity to spot patterns and shifts in system behaviour. As a result, this aids in making predicted adjustments to the control parameters, which in turn reduce system deviations.

- **Robust Performance**: Highly dependable in a wide range of operating circumstances, ACS are built to adapt control settings to unexpected disturbances or changes, allowing for robust operation.

- **Cost-benefit Optimization:** Adaptive controllers help optimise costs by reducing the need for tuning or replacement as the system evolves. This is in contrast to classic control systems, where controllers may require regular tuning or replacement.

- **Automated Learning:** Autonomous learning, the capacity to regulate itself without human input, is a defining feature of adaptive control systems.

- Due to their versatility, robust performance, and capacity to handle system uncertainties, adaptive control systems find extensive use in varied industries like process control, robotics, aerospace, and manufacturing.

Advantages of Adaptive Control Systems

- **Automated Adjustment:** No more tedious hand-tuning is necessary with an adaptive control system because it automatically modifies its settings in response to changes or system behaviour.

- **Improved System Performance:** Maintaining high system performance and overall efficiency is achieved by ACS through continual adjustment to system fluctuations.

- **Proactive Problem Solving:** By quickly modifying control settings in response to changes detected by the system, ACS is able to proactively resolve issues, decrease deviations, and preserve stability.

- **Reduced Maintenance Cost:** Because the system can adjust itself, there's no need to constantly replace or retune the controller, which means less money spent on upkeep.

- **Efficient Learning Mechanism:** In addition to reducing the need for human involvement, a thorough learning process guarantees accurate and resilient operation in varied and dynamic contexts.

Disadvantages of Adaptive Control Systems

- **Complexity:** When compared to other control systems, ACSs are more difficult because of the extensive algorithms and architecture needed to respond to dynamic changes in real-time.

- **Limitations in Rapid Changes:** Because ACS may need some time to adjust to sudden system changes, performance may suffer.

- **Challenges with Large System Uncertainties:** Even if ACS is strong, it may have trouble keeping the system running smoothly when enormous system uncertainties are present.

- **Increased Initial Investment:** The sophisticated characteristics of an adaptive control system cause its price to be higher than that of a traditional control system.

Implementation of Adaptive Control Systems

A well-planned approach is necessary for the successful implementation of adaptive control systems. This approach starts with a comprehensive analysis of the system requirements and continues with the selection of the most suitable ACS for the system. Possible approaches to effectively implementing adaptive control systems include conducting cost-benefit analyses, evaluating vendors, and engaging in thorough planning. Maximising the potential of these dynamic systems is possible with a clearly defined implementation plan and regular monitoring, which allows for efficient and reliable system performance. It is essential to remember that adaptive control systems necessitate ongoing review and improvement since these systems rely on an environment that encourages continual learning and progress.

Finally, by simulating systems that are robust against changes and uncertainties, adaptive control systems are giving industries a leg up thanks to their self-learning capabilities and dynamic adaptability. Enhanced industrial automation and operational efficiency can be achieved through the strategic deployment of these controlled systems and their continuous improvement.

33. Neural Networks and Deep Learning

What we call a "neural network" is actually a model for machine learning that attempts to simulate the way the human brain works by simulating the interactions between neurones in the brain to detect events, assess alternatives, and draw conclusions.

An input layer, a hidden layer (or layers), and an output layer are the three basic components of any neural network. Every node has its own weight and threshold, and it links to other nodes. Nodes are activated and data is sent to the next layer of the network if their outputs exceed a certain threshold. If this is not the case, then no data is transmitted to the subsequent network layer.

In order for neural networks to learn and become more accurate over time, they need training data. Once adjusted for precision, they become potent AI and computer science tools that let us quickly cluster and categorise data. Machine learning tasks in speech and image recognition can be completed in minutes rather than hours, compared to human specialists manually identifying the same objects. The search algorithm used by Google is one of the most well-known applications of neural networks.

How do neural networks work?

Consider the input data, weights, bias (or threshold), and output of each node as a separate linear regression model. Here is an example of how the formula would appear:

$$\sum wixi + bias = w1x1 + w2x2 + w3x3 + bias$$

$$output = f(x) = 1 \text{ if } \sum w1x1 + b >= 0;\ 0 \text{ if } \sum w1x1 + b < 0$$

Weights are assigned when an input layer has been defined. With greater weights contributing more significantly to the output relative to other inputs, these weights assist establish the importance of any particular variable. After that, we multiply each input by its weight and finally add it all up. The activation function then decides the output after passing it through. The node is "fired" (activated) and data is passed on to the next layer of the network if that output surpasses a predetermined threshold. As a consequence, the data sent from one node becomes the data sent to the next node. This type of neural network is called a feedforward network because data is passed from one layer to another.

- Are the waves good? (Yes: 1, No: 0)

- Is the line-up empty? (Yes: 1, No: 0)

- Has there been a recent shark attack? (Yes: 0, No: 1)

Then, let's assume the following, giving us the following inputs:

- X1 = 1, since the waves are pumping

- X2 = 0, since the crowds are out

- X3 = 1, since there hasn't been a recent shark attack

Now, we need to assign some weights to determine importance. Larger weights signify that particular variables are of greater importance to the decision or outcome.

- W1 = 5, since large swells don't come around often

- W2 = 2, since you're used to the crowds

- W3 = 4, since you have a fear of sharks

As a last assumption, we'll use a threshold of 3, which gives us a bias of -3. Now that we have all the necessary inputs, we can begin to input values into the formula in order to obtain the desired output.

Neural networks make use of sigmoid neurones, which are differentiated by having values between 0 and 1, in contrast to the perceptrons used to demonstrate some of the mathematics involved in the previous example. By reducing the effect of a single variable change on the output of any one node and, by extension, the output of the neural network as a whole, x values between 0 and 1 mimic the behaviour of decision trees by cascading input from one node to another.

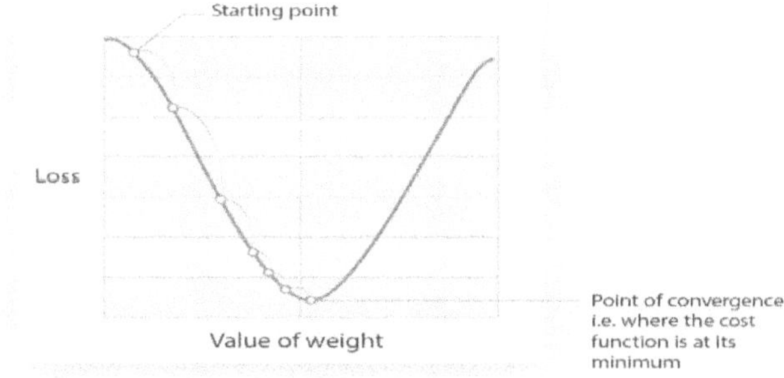

Source: - (IBM, 2021)

<u>Types of neural networks</u>

A variety of forms of neural networks serve specialised functions. This is by no means an exhaustive list of neural network types; nonetheless, the ones listed below are indicative of the most prevalent varieties encountered in practice:

Frank Rosenblatt developed the perceptron in 1958, making it the first neural network. Throughout this piece, we have mostly concentrated on feedforward neural networks, also known as multi-layer perceptrons (MLPs). An input layer, one or more hidden layers, and an output layer make them up. Although MLPs are another name for these neural networks, it's worth noting that most real-world problems aren't linear, therefore these networks actually consist of sigmoid neurones rather than perceptrons. Neural networks, which form the basis of computer vision, NLP, and other applications, are typically trained using data supplied into these models.

While feedforward networks and convolutional neural networks (CNNs) are conceptually similar, CNNs are more commonly used in computer vision, pattern recognition, and image recognition. In order to detect patterns in images, these networks use linear algebraic concepts, especially matrix multiplication.

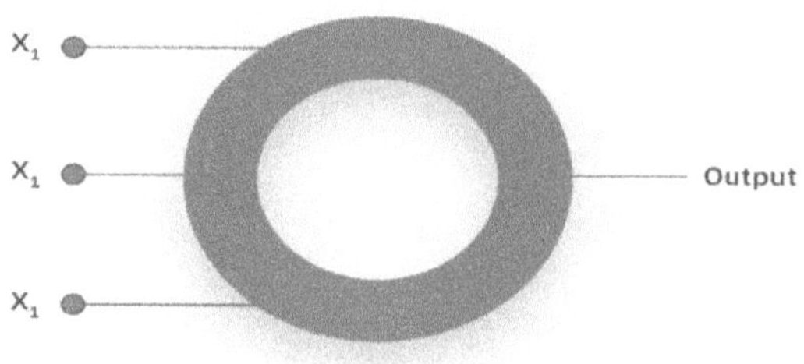

Source: - (IBM, 2021)

Neural networks vs. deep learning

Confusion arises when the terms Deep Learning and neural networks are used interchangeably in everyday speech. So, to clarify, when people talk about "deep learning," what they really mean is the number of layers in a neural network. For the purposes of this article, "deep learning algorithm" refers to a neural network with more than three layers (including inputs and outputs). Neural networks with fewer than three layers are considered to be quite simplistic.

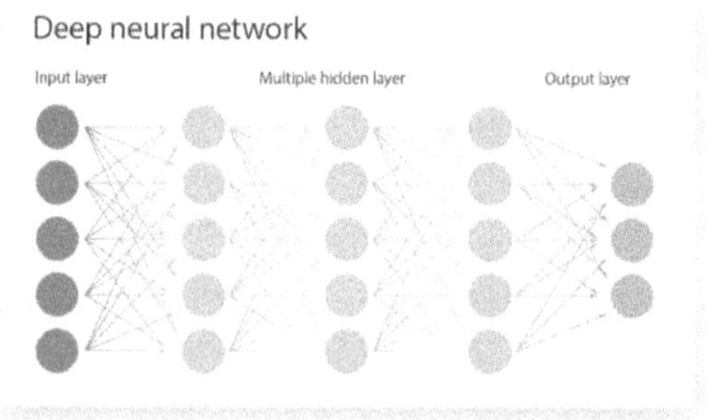

Source: - (IBM, 2021)

33.1. Evolutionary Neural Network Design

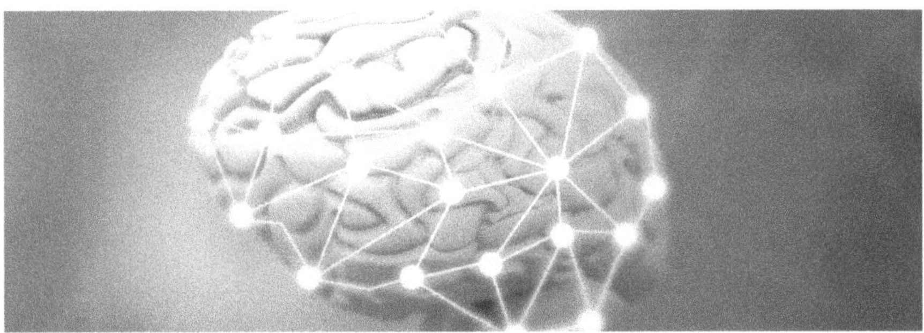

Source: - (admin, 2020)

The field known as "artificial intelligence" (AI) studies how to program computers to act like humans by integrating theoretical and technological ideas from several fields.

This study looks at ways to train deep neural network architectures using evolutionary algorithms to improve pattern categorisation. Neuroevolutionary algorithms enable training of sections of the deep neural network, which is a major benefit of evolutionary algorithms over backpropagation. The present work's framework is flexible enough to accommodate various application scenarios by adjusting to the memory and processor resources needed by the target hardware platform.

"Convolutional Neural Networks" (CNN) are a subset of deep learning neural networks that attempt to replicate the behaviour of the image processing industry's basic convolution operation. Applying evolutionary computation (EC) methods to evolve CNN topologies or kernel weights has recently been the subject of much research.

Convolutional neural networks can skip the feature design step, but adding more and more data makes them more complicated. Three primary features of neural networks—learning techniques, network architecture (topology, transfer function), and network link weights—have been subjected to evolutionary computation methodologies. The current study can be used as a general method to decrease the total size of a deep learning neural network.

33.2. Hyperparameter Optimization

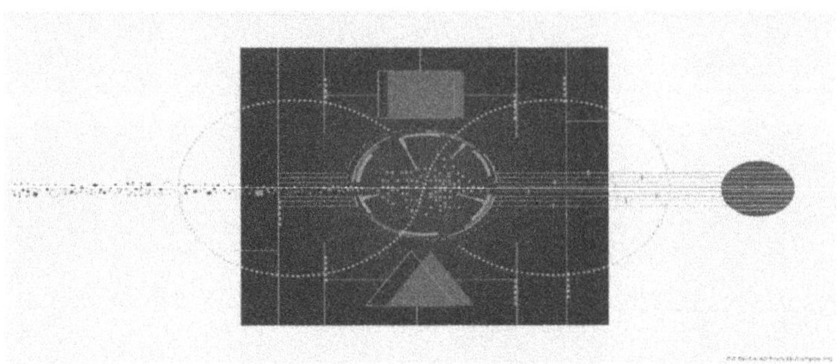

Source: - (Tübingen, 2024)

Chapter Summary The quality of performance of a Machine Learning model heavily depends on its hyperparameter settings. Given a dataset and a task, the choice of the machine learning (ML) model and its hyperparameters is typically performed manually. Hyperparameter Optimization (HPO) algorithms aim to alleviate this task as much as possible for the human expert.

The design of an HPO algorithm depends on the nature of the task and its context, such as the optimization budget and available information. Below are some of the different flavors of performing HPO

- **Combined Algorithms Selection and Hyperparameter Optimization (CASH)**

  Not only does an AutoML system have to decide which model to use, but it must also choose the best hyperparameter configuration for that model. You might think of this issue as a hierarchical problem-solving optimisation (HPO) issue with a configuration space for the top-level hyperparameter, which determines the algorithm to use and is dependent on all the other hyperparameters. We use random forests as surrogate models in Bayesian optimisation, for instance, to handle such structured and complicated configuration spaces.

  Our Packages

  - ○ Auto-sklearn provides out-of-the-box supervised machine learning by modeling the search space as a CASH problem.

- Auto-Pytorch is a framework for automatically searching neural network architecture and its hyperparameters and also makes use of structured configuration space.

- SMAC implements a random forest as a surrogate model which can efficiently deal with structured search spaces.

- **Using many-fidelities for early-stopping HPO**

  The black-box view adopted by Bayesian Optimization can be relaxed with a gray-box view, which allows access to intermediate states of a targeted machine-learning model. That is, the function to be optimized has a proxy state along one or more variables (fidelities) that can be obtained at a cheaper cost and likely indicates the performance of the target state. HPO algorithms that can leverage search over fidelities can provide better anytime performance.

- **Speeding up HPO with learning curves extrapolation techniques**

  Various machine learning algorithms that are trained iteratively yield learning curves. Under different hyperparameter settings, different learning curves can be obtained. Exploiting the smooth trends of a learning curve from a partially trained machine learning model to predict future performance is an active area of research with promising results

- **HPO with expert prior inputs**

  Although HPO can be seen as removing the human from the loop, the intuition and experience of the human expert offer valuable information as a guide for an HPO algorithm. The challenge then is to find suitable interfaces and principled methodologies to realize practical algorithms.

- **Benchmarks for reproducible research**

  There are a lot of obstacles to overcome when evaluating AutoML, and particularly HPO. For instance, it isn't always obvious which benchmarks are emblematic of common HPO applications, running HPO many times might be computationally costly, and the benchmarks themselves can be rather noisy. In order to alleviate researchers' computing strain and increase reproducibility, we create HPO benchmark sets.

34. *Data Mining and Pattern Recognition*

In the realm of artificial intelligence (AI) automation, ML, data mining, and pattern recognition are extremely foundational subjects. Due to people's lack of technical expertise, the methodologies and intentions behind these three domains cause a great deal of confusion. They are all essential components of the modern digital era, contributing to the smooth operation of businesses and the development of new technologies. These three areas are crucial for many industries to succeed and overcome obstacles that impact their global operations and growth. Anyone interested in these fields professionally or just wants to know more about the differences between them will find this material very useful.

- **Pattern Recognition**

  This area of artificial intelligence gained traction in the '50s. Researchers and practitioners alike were showing an interest in building systems for optical character and speech recognition about this period. Researchers and practitioners in this area work on creating and implementing systems that can detect and classify patterns in data, whether it be pictures, signals, objects, or processes, by means of various sensing techniques. Pattern recognition enables distinct and strategic advantages for industries, enabling continuous improvement and evolution. A strategic edge in this dynamic world would describe this. Data is first segmented, and then differentiated, using distinct algorithms to help with the process based on predetermined criteria or common elements. As a result, there is potential for development in this core area of machine learning. In order to create tales or knowledge from data represented by flat lines, spikes, flows, and ebbs, pattern recognition is an essential component of machine learning technology. The information gathered might be presented as text, graphics, or audio.

The Process of Pattern Recognition

- Gathering data from sources via tracking or inputs.

- Swabbing of data from noise.

- Scrutinization of information retrieved to form relevant elements and characteristics.

- Grouping of the features/ elements.

- Examination of categories/ classes, therefore, generating sets of data.

- Execution of derived insights to facilitate industrial or business operations.

<u>Applications of Pattern Recognition</u>

- Optical Character Recognition: It is used in processing handwritten materials, documents, signatures, and text transcription.

- Processing of Natural Language: This includes text analysis, transcription, and generation. For instance, in plagiarism detection and translation of one language to the other.

- Data analysis: For instance, forecasting the stock market using comparative studies to generate and predict the possible outcomes.

- **Machine Learning**

Machine learning (ML) is a subfield of artificial intelligence that teaches computers to sift through massive datasets in search of patterns that will allow them to make predictions and draw conclusions. Computers can understand and interpret the data provided without any human involvement. Machine learning (ML) is the process of teaching computers to analyse data and perform tasks in a manner similar to a human. Accurate predictions that aid in decision-making can be gathered in this way. In machine learning, the goal is to educate the computer to recognise certain things in photos, people, or any other type of data. For instance, in order to build autonomous vehicles that can perceive and analyse everything in their immediate vicinity, improving both safety and efficiency, a computer may be programmed to learn about traffic items and concepts.

Clustering algorithms, regression, semi-supervised learning, Bayesian learning algorithms, and supervised learning are some of the more minor varieties of ML. Computer systems are introduced to many sets of labelled data through supervised learning. In this learning process, the computer learns to recognise handwritten figures by locating groups of pixels and other forms that are associated with each one. Unsupervised learning, on the other side, is all about finding patterns in data. By classifying information, the system is trained to recognise patterns. Data mining models and other types of training data/algorithms are ultimately used by ML to create models for future predictions. With the help of preexisting data and techniques, ML got its start in the 1950s.

Applications of Machine Learning

- Neural networks

- Computer vision

- Web-search

- Fraud detection and credit scoring

- Spam filter

- Computer design and other cognitive services.

- **Data Mining**

The goal of data mining and knowledge discovery is to extract useful information from massive amounts of data kept in repositories like databases and data warehouses. It had its beginnings earlier, but it wasn't until the 1990s that it was made perfect with the help of humans. In the corporate world in particular, data mining is useful for making decisions. Regression, clustering, decision trees, and sequential pattern analysis are some of the methods used in this procedure. It relies on mining large datasets for previously unknown insights and best practices. Images, videos, and other types of raw data are automatically processed to extract the data, which is then used to generate reports. Businesses subsequently utilise the reports for decision-making purposes. By gathering data and retrieving pertinent information, businesses can find trends and patterns. Data mining's ability to discover previously unseen patterns via categorisation and sequence analysis makes it crucial.

Data Mining Steps

- Mining

- Modeling

- Evaluation of pattern

- Presentation of Knowledge

Data Mining Processing

- Acquisition of data

- Cleaning of data

- Reduction of data

- Transformation of data

Applications of Data Mining

- Telecommunication firms

- Intrusion prevention and detection

- Financial data analysis

34.1. Feature Selection and Extraction

Many industries have been drastically changed by the rapid use of machine learning. It enables companies to derive useful insights from data and make well-informed decisions. Improving the efficacy and efficiency of machine learning models relies heavily on two principal approaches, namely feature selection and feature engineering. To optimise predictive models in this age of exponential data expansion, it is crucial to extract useful features from massive datasets.

A survey carried out by CrowdFlower revealed that 80 data scientists devoted a considerable amount of time, almost 60%, to the vital responsibility of cleaning and organising data. The significance of having knowledge in engineering and feature selection is shown by this discovery.

When it comes to boosting model accuracy, decreasing overfitting, and enhancing computing efficiency, feature selection is absolutely critical. Feature engineering allows models to effectively capture key patterns by turning raw data into meaningful representations. These techniques are incredibly critical for effective analysis in today's data landscape, which is characterised by tremendous volume (about 328.77 million terabytes generated daily) and complexity. Feature selection and engineering are two of machine learning's most fundamental ideas, and this article delves into both.

What is Feature Engineering

Feature engineering is picking and changing variables or features in your dataset with care. All the while, the predictive model is being built using machine learning techniques. A prerequisite to successfully training your machine learning algorithms is extracting features from the raw dataset you have collected. Prior to the training process, this stage allows for data preparation and organisation.

Otherwise, gaining valuable insights from your data could prove challenging. The process of feature engineering serves two primary objectives:

- Providing a compatible input dataset for machine learning algorithms.

- Modelling machine learning to improve performance.

Imputation

Feature engineering entails fixing problems including invalid data, missing values, human mistake, general blunders, and insufficient data sources. A missing value can have a major effect on how well an algorithm works. We employ a method called "imputation" to deal with this problem. When dealing with dataset irregularities, imputation is a lifesaver.

- **Handling Outliers:** Data points or values that differ greatly from the rest of the data are called outliers, and they have a negative effect on the model's performance. Finding and then eliminating these erroneous values is what this method is all about. A data set's outliers can be better understood with the use of the standard deviation. To elaborate, there is a predetermined distance from the average for each value in the dataset. An outlier, on the other hand, is a value that deviates greatly from a predetermined threshold. The Z-score is another tool for finding outliers.

- **Log transform:** A common mathematical tool in machine learning is the log transform, which is also called the logarithm transformation. Data analysis and moderation are two areas that benefit from its many uses. The capacity to handle skewed data is a major plus, since it changes the distribution so that it closely matches a normal distribution. In addition to improving model robustness, the log transform helps reduce the effect of outliers on datasets by normalising magnitude differences.

- **Binning:** Problems with overfitting, which can severely damage model performance, are common in machine learning. When data is noisy and there are too many parameters, overfitting happens. In feature engineering, this effective method is known as "binning," and it can assist normalise the noisy data. It entails sorting various characteristics into predetermined categories.

- **Feature Split:** Feature splitting is the process of adding new features by breaking existing ones into several smaller ones.

Improved pattern recognition within the dataset is made possible by this method, which also improves algorithmic understanding. New features are more able to be clustered and binned through the feature splitting process. In the end, this boosts data model performance and leads to the extraction of useful information.

What is Feature Selection?

By utilising only relevant data and eliminating any unnecessary noise from the dataset, feature selection reduces the number of input variables in the model. Machine learning is the automated selection of features that are most relevant to a given problem and used to train a model to address that problem. Here, key elements are either kept intact or included or excluded deliberately. This reduces the amount and breadth of the input dataset while effectively eliminating irrelevant noise.

Feature Selection Techniques

Feature selection incorporates various popular techniques, namely filter methods, wrapper methods, and embedded methods.

Filter Methods

In the preprocessing stage, relevant features are selected using filter methods, independent of any particular machine learning algorithm. By removing correlated and superfluous features, they improve computing efficiency and effectiveness. Be warned, though; multicollinearity is something they might not handle. The following are examples of frequently used filter methods:

- **Chi-square test:** By comparing the observed and predicted values, the Chi-square Test investigates the relationship between categorical variables. If you want to find major correlations between data set attributes, you need this statistical technique.

- **Fisher's Score:** The Fisher criterion is used to independently pick each characteristic. The relevance of features is increased when their Fisher's scores are higher.

- **Corelation coefficient:** You may measure the strength and direction of a relationship between two continuous variables using the correlation coefficient. The Pearson's Correlation Coefficient is a popular tool for feature selection.

Wrapper Methods

Iteratively training the model with different subsets of features is the goal of wrapper methods, also called greedy algorithms. They assess how well the model is doing and make adjustments to its features as needed. Although they demand a lot of processing power, wrapper methods provide an ideal collection of features. Methods for wrapping things up often make use of the following techniques:

- To begin, the model is trained with a blank slate of features using Forward Selection, which iteratively integrates the feature that yields the highest performance gain.

- Combining forward selection and backward elimination techniques simultaneously, Bi-directional Elimination achieves a unique solution.

- To get the target number of features, the Recursive Elimination approach assesses progressi

34.2. Classification and Regression

Classification and regression are the two main prediction issues in data mining. The most fundamental distinction between regression and classification algorithms is that the former deals with continuous real values and the latter with discrete ones.

Either a real number or a continuous type of output is required. For classification to work, the output variable must have a discrete value. On the other hand, for regression to work, the output variable can only take on real or continuous values.

Here we'll go over the key distinctions between regression and classification. First, we'll go over the fundamentals of Classification and Regression to help you grasp their differences.

What is Classification

Objects whose class label is anonymous can be predicted using a model that represents and differentiates data classes or concepts; this process is known as classification. Training records, or data objects with known class labels, provide the basis of the generated model.

Classification explains the act of assigning instances predetermined class labels based on their qualities; it is one of the most significant ideas in data mining. Classification is a predefined approach to effective analysis of large datasets.

What is Regression

Any continuous-valued attribute can be forecasted using regression, a supervised machine learning approach. Some commercial organisations can use regression to investigate the relationships between the goal variable and the predictor variables. Therefore, regression is a crucial tool for investigating data for financial forecasting and time series modelling. Classification can be accomplished by the use of regression. Two techniques, division and prediction, are employed for this purpose. While prediction makes use of certain formulae to forecast the class's output value, division involves dividing the data into regions based on the class.

For some dependent datasets, regression can provide predictions. In addition to supporting methods for variable prediction, regression also relies on specific assumptions and constraints, such as the independence of variables and their inherent normal distributions. Discover our most recent online courses and gain knowledge at your own speed. If you want to advance in your career, enrol and get your expert certification. Classification offers a prediction model that uses historical data to forecast new data in discrete labels, whereas regression predicts data in continuous values; this is the main distinction between the two.

35. *Chapter Summary*

By combining AI and NFC technology, the NextGen Library system streamlines operations, meets the needs of modern users, and completely changes the game when it comes to traditional library management. By utilising real-time responses and personalised recommendations, this novel approach improves user interaction, inventory management, and transaction processes with NFC. Maximising or minimising functions under restrictions are examples of calculus optimisation issues that are important in many applications, including scheduling and manufacturing. For example, logistics route scheduling takes client schedules and driver availability into account to optimise delivery routes and increase efficiency. In addition, optimising hyperparameters to reduce validation errors is part of parameter tuning in predictive models like PROC GRADBOOST. The significance of efficient and adaptable solutions in a world driven by technology is shown by these developments in mathematical optimisation, logistics, and library administration.

Size, domain of application, purpose, and operational style are four ways to classify robots. Large robots, such as those utilised in construction and manufacturing, carry out labour-intensive operations, while smaller and medium-sized robots, like those found in homes and toys, are ubiquitous in everyday life. Personal robots are designed for individual usage, while industrial robots are used for specialised jobs. Another way to classify robots is by application domain. According to purpose-based classification, there are two types of robots: those built specifically for performing a single function, and those that can be modified to perform a wide range of jobs. From an operational standpoint, robots can do various duties either alone, in small groups, or even in swarms. In the past, ideas like the golem and automation sparked a quest to build robots with human-like characteristics and skills, and today, robotics has evolved to mirror this goal.

Both possibilities and worries arise from the advancement and incorporation of robots into human civilisation. Robots, on the one hand, can automate and streamline a lot of processes, which is a huge plus in many different industries. Concerns regarding their possible displacement of human workers and changes to control dynamics in the labour market continue to be a source of persistent anxiety. On top of that, when robots get more lifelike, humans may have trouble seeing and trusting them, which can lead to awkward or confused interactions.

Taking cues from Alan Turing's concept of artificial evolution, evolutionary robotics aims to empower robots to autonomously design and enhance subsequent generations by utilising developments in 3D printing, neural networks, and adaptive control systems. Adaptive control systems (ACS) are complicated and might have trouble keeping up with fast changes, but they improve performance by responding to input and system changes in real-time, which has benefits including automated adjustment and cost savings. Neural networks have great promise for improving AI capabilities and efficiency; they analyse input through interconnected nodes to accomplish tasks like voice and picture recognition, replicating the human brain.

takes a look at the many facets of robotics, neural networks, and ML methods, showcasing the latest developments and uses in these fields. The article starts out by talking about how robots could evolve; essentially, how they could use evolutionary algorithms to create new generations of robots without human intervention. Drawing on Alan Turing's original concepts, this approach makes use of cutting-edge technology such as neural networks and 3D printing. Next, we'll go over adaptive control systems, which can improve system performance in a variety of industries by making real-time adjustments based on feedback. The varieties of neural networks, including perceptrons, feedforward networks, and convolutional neural networks (CNNs), are described with an emphasis on their uses in deep learning and pattern recognition. Included in the discussion are topics such as feature selection and engineering, hyperparameter optimisation (HPO), and the automation of machine learning model tuning. In conclusion, it differentiates data mining's classification and regression methods, explaining how each can be applied to forecast both continuous and discrete values.

Part 1: (Very Short Questions)

1. What are the key challenges in scheduling and routing optimization problems?

2. How can parameter tuning improve machine learning model performance?

3. What is evolutionary robotics and how does it differ from traditional robotics?

4. What role does adaptive control play in modern automation systems?

5. How can evolutionary algorithms contribute to neural network design?

6. What are common methods for hyperparameter optimization in deep learning?

7. How does feature selection impact data mining outcomes?

8. What techniques are used for feature extraction in pattern recognition?

9. How do classification and regression tasks differ in data mining?

10. What are the benefits of combining evolutionary strategies with neural networks?

Part 2: (Short Questions)

1. What are some common techniques used for scheduling and routing in optimization problems?

2. How does evolutionary robotics differ from traditional robotics in terms of design and adaptation?

3. What methods are commonly used for hyperparameter optimization in neural network models?

4. What are the primary approaches for feature selection and extraction in data mining?

5. How can parameter tuning impact the performance of machine learning algorithms?

Part 3: (Long Questions)

1. How can optimization techniques be applied to complex scheduling and routing problems in logistics and transportation?

2. What are the key strategies for parameter tuning and configuration in machine learning models?

3. How does evolutionary robotics contribute to the development of adaptive control systems?

4. What are the current methodologies for designing and optimizing neural networks, including the role of evolutionary algorithms in neural network architecture design?

5. How do data mining techniques assist in feature selection and extraction, and what impact do these techniques have on pattern recognition tasks?

Part 4: (MCQs)

1. Which of the following is a common objective in optimization problems related to scheduling?

   a. Minimizing training time of a neural network

   b. Maximizing the efficiency of routing algorithms

   c. Reducing the number of tasks completed

   d. Optimizing the number of machine learning feature

2. In parameter tuning for machine learning models, what is the primary goal?

   a. To increase the number of parameters

   b. To reduce the number of features

   c. To improve model performance by finding the optimal parameter values

   d. To select the most complex model

3. Which technique is most commonly used in evolutionary robotics?

   a. Genetic algorithms

   b. Gradient descent

   c. K-means clustering

   d. Principal component analysis

4. What is the primary focus of adaptive control systems in robotics?

   a. Designing static control laws

   b. Adjusting control parameters in real-time based on system performance

   c. Reducing the computational complexity of robotic tasks

   d. Increasing the physical strength of robots

5. In the context of neural networks, what does "evolutionary neural network design" involve?

   a. Using neural networks to evolve new algorithms

   b. Applying genetic algorithms to optimize neural network structures

   c. Evolving neural network weights during training

   d. Designing networks based on evolution theory

6. Which method is typically used for hyperparameter optimization in deep learning?

   a. Grid search

   b. Principal component analysis

   c. Feature selection

   d. K-nearest neighbors

7. In data mining, what is the purpose of feature selection and extraction?

   a. To reduce the number of features while retaining essential information

   b. To increase the number of features for better model complexity

   c. To select irrelevant features for better performance

   d. To improve the speed of data collection

8. Which algorithm is commonly used for classification tasks in data mining?

   a. K-means clustering

   b. Decision Trees

   c. Principal Component Analysis

   d. Gaussian Mixture Models

9. What is the main goal of regression analysis in data mining?

   a. To categorize data into classes

   b. To predict continuous numerical values

   c. To extract features from data

   d. To reduce data dimensionality

10. Which technique is used for routing optimization in logistics?

   a. K-means clustering

   b. Genetic algorithms

   c. Ant colony optimization

   d. Principal component analysis

Answer

1	2	3	4	5	6	7	8	9	10
b	c	a	b	b	a	a	b	b	c

Bibliography

Adams, D. (2023). *Mechanisms of Natural Selection.* https://open. baypath.edu/bsc109/chapter/kp-6-4a/

admin. (2020). *Evolutionary Design of Deep Neural Networks.* Ness Digital Engineering. https://www.ness.com/evolutionary-design-of-deep-neural-networks/

Alizadeh Foroutan, R., Shafipour, M., Rezaeian, J., & Khojasteh, Y. (2023). Just-in-time scheduling of unrelated parallel machines with family setups and soft time window constraints. *Journal of Industrial and Production Engineering*, 1–24. https://doi.org/10.1080/21681015 .2024.2361046

Andrei, F. (2024). *Efficient feature selection via CMA-ES (Covariance Matrix Adaptation Evolution Strategy).* Medium. https://towardsdatascience.com/ efficient-feature-selection-via-cma-es-covariance-matrix-adaptation-evolution-strategy-ee312bc7b173

Awotunde, J. B., Matiluko, O. E., & Fatai, O. W. (2014). *Medical Diagnosis System Using Fuzzy Logic.* 7(2).

Bennefall, P. (2016). *How to perform rank based selection in a genetic algorithm?* [Forum post]. Stack Overflow. https://stackoverflow. com/q/20290831

Bentley, P. (2024). *Aspects of Evolutionary Design by Computers by Peter Bentley.* http://www0.cs.ucl.ac.uk/staff/P.Bentley/wc3paper

bgiservice. (2024). *Data Representation.* BGI SERVICE. https://www. bgiservice.in/data-representation/

Biswas, A. (2020). *Introduction to Evolution Strategy.* Medium. https://towardsdatascience.com/introduction-to-evolution-strategy-1b78b9d48385

BrainKart. (2023). *Basics of Mechanisms.* BrainKart. https://www.brainkart.com/article/Basics-of-Mechanisms_6269/

Brand, S. (2023). *WHAT IS YOUR FAVORITE DEEP, ELEGANT, OR BEAUTIFUL EXPLANATION?* https://www.edge.org/response-detail/11843

Cifci, M. A. (2023). NP-hard Problems. *Medium.* https://themanoftalent.medium.com/np-hard-problems-218852451488a

Diem Redux. (2015). *Swarm Robotics, by Diem Redux.* Diem Redux. https://diemredux.bandcamp.com/track/swarm-robotics

D'souza, R. N., Huang, P.-Y., & Yeh, F.-C. (2020). Structural Analysis and Optimization of Convolutional Neural Networks with a Small Sample Size. *Scientific Reports, 10,* 834. https://doi.org/10.1038/s41598-020-57866-2

Dubetcky, O. (2024). Resource Constraints Task in Google OR-Tools with Fuzzy Logic (Coding). *Medium.* https://oleg-dubetcky.medium.com/resource-constraints-task-in-google-or-tools-with-fuzzy-logic-coding-4fe7938a7c65

Erten, S. (2023). *Figure 1: Modularity based phylogenetic analysis of molecular...* ResearchGate. https://www.researchgate.net/figure/Modularity-based-phylogenetic-analysis-of-molecular-interaction-networks_fig2_228691213

Fogel, D. B. (2010). Revisiting Overlooked Foundations of Evolutionary Computation: Part I. *Cybernetics and Systems, 41*(5), 343–358. https://doi.org/10.1080/01969722.2010.486222

GeeksforGeeks. (2018). *Tournament Selection (GA).* GeeksforGeeks. https://www.geeksforgeeks.org/tournament-selection-ga/

GeeksforGeeks. (2019). *Crossover in Genetic Algorithm.* GeeksforGeeks. https://www.geeksforgeeks.org/crossover-in-genetic-algorithm/

Gómez, F. (2023). Genetic algorithms for feature selection in machine learning. *Neural Designer*. https://www.neuraldesigner.com/blog/genetic_algorithms_for_feature_selection/

Healthcare Robot. (2024). *Case Studies | Healthcare Robot | Cleaning robot and more.* Healthcare Robot. https://www.hospital-robots.com/post/evolutionary-robotics

Hughes, P. (2020). *Application Challenges in a Real-Time World | Nordic APIs |.* Nordic APIs. https://nordicapis.com/application-challenges-in-a-real-time-world/

IBM. (2021). *What is a Neural Network? | IBM.* https://www.ibm.com/topics/neural-networks

Jin, S., Fan, X., Stamper, C., Mole, R. A., Yu, Y., Hong, L., Yu, D., & Baggioli, M. (2024). On the temperature dependence of the density of states of liquids at low energies. *Scientific Reports*, *14*(1), 18805. https://doi.org/10.1038/s41598-024-69504-2

Kamboj, J. (2024, April 1). The Role of AI in Data Analytics: Transforming Decision-Making. *Imenso Software*. https://www.imensosoftware.com/blog/ai-in-data-analytics-transforming-decision-making/

Kassahun, Y., Edgington, M., Metzen, J., Sommer, G., & Kirchner, F. (2007). *A common genetic encoding for both direct and indirect encodings of networks.* https://doi.org/10.1145/1276958.1277162

Kumar, M., & Garg, D. (2005). Neuro-fuzzy control applied to multiple cooperating robots. *Industrial Robot: An International Journal*, *32*, 234–239. https://doi.org/10.1108/01439910510593929

Kumar, V., & Yadav, S. M. (2022). A state-of-the-Art review of heuristic and metaheuristic optimization techniques for the management of water resources. *Water Supply*, *22*(4), 3702–3728. https://doi.org/10.2166/ws.2022.010

Li, G., Zhang, X., Zhao, J., Zhang, H., Ye, J., & Zhang, W. (2013). A Self-Adaptive Parameter Optimization Algorithm in a Real-Time Parallel Image Processing System. *The Scientific World Journal*, *2013*, 978548. https://doi.org/10.1155/2013/978548

Lin, W.-Y., Lee, W.-Y., & Hong, T.-P. (2003). Adapting Crossover and Mutation Rates in Genetic Algorithms. *J. Inf. Sci. Eng., 19*, 889–903.

Llanes, A., Muñoz, A., Bueno-Crespo, A., García-Valverde, T., Sánchez, A., Arcas-Túnez, F., Pérez-Sánchez, H., & M. Cecilia, J. (2016). Soft Computing Techniques for the Protein Folding Problem on High Performance Computing Architectures. *Current Drug Targets, 17*(14), 1626–1648. https://doi.org/10.2174/138945011766 6160201114028

Matchaya, G., Malambo, M., & Mayoyo, A. (2024). *Enabling environment and digital technology use readiness in agriculture in the Zambezi riparian countries.*

Melin, P., & Castillo, O. (2005). *Hybrid Intelligent Systems for Pattern Recognition Using Soft Computing—An Evolutionary Approach for Neural Networks and Fuzzy Systems.* https://doi.org/10.1007/b97585

Mignon, J. (2020). *Complex Adaptative System—Key Characteristics.* Pentalog. https://www.pentalog.com/blog/strategy/complex-adaptive-systems/

Mohan, B. (2022). *Fig.8. Pie chart showing personality percentage.* ResearchGate. https://www.researchgate.net/figure/Pie-chart-showing-personality-percentage_fig4_366660416

Moon, C., Lee, Y. H., Jeong, C. S., & Yun, Y. (2008). Integrated process planning and scheduling in a supply chain. *Computers & Industrial Engineering, 54*(4), 1048–1061. https://doi.org/10.1016/j.cie.2007.06.018

Moretti, E. de A., Anholon, R., Rampasso, I. S., Silva, D., Santa-Eulalia, L. A., & Ignácio, P. S. de A. (2024). Main difficulties during RFID implementation: An exploratory factor analysis approach. *Technology Analysis & Strategic Management, 31*(8), 943–956. https://doi.org/10.1080/09537325.2019.1575351

MSc, F. B. (2024). Rewriting the Rules of the Game: How Artificial Intelligence and Game Theory Work Together. *Medium.* https://medium.com/@fatihbildirici.dev/rewriting-the-rules-of-the-game-how-artificial-intelligence-and-game-theory-work-together-a62e545eb1b6

Nasir, M., Lim, C. P., Nahavandi, S., & Creighton, D. (2024). Prediction of pedestrians routes within a built environment in normal conditions. *Expert Systems with Applications, 41*(10), 4975–4988. https://doi.org/10.1016/j.eswa.2014.02.034

Oreilly. (2024). *The x86 Architecture—Practical Malware Analysis [Book].* https://www.oreilly.com/library/view/practical-malware-analysis/9781593272906/ch05s03.html

Prathima. (2021). What is Reinforcement Learning and How Does It Work (Updated 2024). *Analytics Vidhya.* https://www.analyticsvidhya.com/blog/2021/02/introduction-to-reinforcement-learning-for-beginners/

Rathinam, J. (2024). *Optimization and design analysis.* https://www.linkedin.com/pulse/optimization-design-analysis-janaga-rathinam-yethc

Royal Berglee, P. (2016). *2.2 Historical Development Patterns.* https://open.lib.umn.edu/worldgeography/chapter/2-2-historical-development-patterns/

Sakhuja, S. (2024). Gradient-Based vs. Gradient-Free Optimization. *Medium.* https://sakhujasaiyam.medium.com/gradient-based-vs-gradient-free-optimization-82fa7e90b3e9

Schrader, J. (2020). *Adaptive Intelligence: What the World Needs Right Now | Psychology Today.* https://www.psychologytoday.com/us/blog/successful-intelligence/202009/adaptive-intelligence-what-the-world-needs-right-now

Silaich, S., & Gupta, S. (2023). Feature Selection in High Dimensional Data: A Review. In S. Kumar, H. Sharma, K. Balachandran, J. H. Kim, & J. C. Bansal (Eds.), *Third Congress on Intelligent Systems* (pp. 703–717). Springer Nature. https://doi.org/10.1007/978-981-19-9225-4_51

Sipper, M., Fu, W., Ahuja, K., & Moore, J. H. (2018). Investigating the parameter space of evolutionary algorithms. *BioData Mining, 11*(1), 2. https://doi.org/10.1186/s13040-018-0164-x

Søreide, K. (2024). Numbers needed to tweet: Social media and impact on surgery. *European Journal of Surgical Oncology, 45*(2), 292–295. https://doi.org/10.1016/j.ejso.2018.10.054

Spears, W. (1998). *Adapting Crossover in Evolutionary Algorithms*.

SrmiSTAdmiNrmp. (2024). 5 DAYS ONLINE FACULTY DEVELOPMENT PROGRAMME ON "INTEGRATION OF ADVANCED TECHNOLOGIES TO INDUSTRY 4.0." *SRM Ramapuram | SRMIST Ramapuram*. https://srmrmp.edu.in/5-days-online-faculty-development-programme-on-integration-of-advanced-technologies-to-industry-4-0/

Stokkebye, A. (2022). *What is the Fitness Evaluation?* Hoag Executive Health. https://hoagexecutivehealth.com/exercise-physiology/what-is-the-fitness-evaluation/

Tai, K., El-Sayed, A.-R., Biglarbegian, M., Gonzalez, C. I., Castillo, O., & Mahmud, S. (2016). Review of Recent Type-2 Fuzzy Controller Applications. *Algorithms*, *9*(2), Article 2. https://doi.org/10.3390/a9020039

Tatiwar, R. (2023, December 1). Neuroevolution: Evolving Neural Network with Genetic Algorithms. *Medium*. https://medium.com/@roopal.tatiwar20/neuroevolution-evolving-neural-network-with-genetic-algorithms-8ca2165ad04c

Tübingen. (2024). *AutoML | Hyperparameter Optimization*. https://www.automl.org/hpo-overview/

Tutorialspoint. (2024). *Genetic Algorithms—Introduction*. https://www.tutorialspoint.com/genetic_algorithms/genetic_algorithms_introduction.htm

Upadhyay, V. (2024). *Introsort Screen | PDF | Algorithms And Data Structures | Algorithms*. Scribd. https://www.scribd.com/document/349509743/Introsort-Screen

Vikhar, P. A. (2024). Evolutionary algorithms: A critical review and its future prospects. *2016 International Conference on Global Trends in Signal Processing, Information Computing and Communication (ICGTSPICC)*, 261–265. 2016 International Conference on Global Trends in Signal Processing, Information Computing and Communication (ICGTSPICC). https://doi.org/10.1109/ICGTSPICC.2016.7955308